The Battle of Cannae: The History and Legacy Decisive Military Defe:

By Charles River Editors

A depiction of Hannibal crossing the Alps during the Second Punic War

About Charles River Editors

Charles River Editors provides superior editing and original writing services across the digital publishing industry, with the expertise to create digital content for publishers across a vast range of subject matter. In addition to providing original digital content for third party publishers, we also republish civilization's greatest literary works, bringing them to new generations of readers via ebooks.

Sign up here to receive updates about free books as we publish them, and visit Our Kindle Author Page to browse today's free promotions and our most recently published Kindle titles.

Introduction

Jorg Schulz's picture of a modern monument near the battlefield

The Battle of Cannae

"Few battles of ancient times are more marked by ability...than the battle of Cannae. The position was such as to place every advantage on Hannibal's side. The manner in which the far from perfect Hispanic and Gallic foot was advanced in a wedge in échelon...was first held there and then withdrawn step by step, until it had reached the converse position...is a simple masterpiece of battle tactics. The advance at the proper moment of the African infantry, and its wheel right and left upon the flanks of the disordered and crowded Roman legionaries, is far beyond praise. The whole battle, from the Carthaginian standpoint, is a consummate piece of art, having no superior, few equal, examples in the history of war." – Theodore Dodge, military historian

Although the Romans gained the upper hand over Carthage in the wake of the First Punic War, the legendary Carthaginian general Hannibal brought the Romans to their knees for over a decade during the Second Punic War. While military historians are still amazed that he was able to maintain his army in Italy near Rome for nearly 15 years, scholars are still puzzled over some of his decisions, including why he never attempted to march on Rome in the first place.

Regardless, Hannibal was such a threat that the Romans responded in an unprecedented nature when the Carthaginians resumed the campaigning season in the spring of 216 BCE by capturing the city of Cannae, a crucial supply hub, and placing themselves along the line that convoys from the ports and warehouses of the south needed to travel to reach Rome. This was something the Romans could not and did not take lying down; Rome raised the largest army in their city's history, a force of between 80,000 and 100,000 men, and marched south with Consuls Varro and Paullus at the head of the army. This military behemoth disregarded the delaying tactics that Maximus had favored, fully determined to destroy Hannibal once and for all as quickly as possible. Polybius described the incredible size of this Roman army: "The Senate determined to bring eight legions into the field, which had never been done at Rome before, each legion consisting of five thousand men besides allies. ...Most of their wars are decided by one consul and two legions, with their quota of allies; and they rarely employ all four at one time and on one service. But on this occasion, so great was the alarm and terror of what would happen, they resolved to bring not only four but eight legions into the field."

Despite the massive horde headed his way, Hannibal was ready for them. He encamped his army near the Aufidus, a river not far from Cannae, and waited. His intelligence told him that Consul Varro, the more influential of the two Roman generals, was a firebrand, talented in attack but with a tendency to overreach himself, and Hannibal resolved to use this flaw to his advantage. Hannibal arrayed his army in the open, sure that Varro would be unable to resist the temptation to offer battle, and then deliberately placed his weakest infantry in the center of his battle-line. Varro led the Roman legions straight at the centre of Hannibal's formation, proceeding in characteristic bull-headed fashion and spearheading the assault himself. Hannibal's troops in the center yielded before the legions, as Hannibal had anticipated, sucking the bulk of the Roman force deep into the centre of Hannibal's formation. Meanwhile, the wings of Hannibal's infantry automatically swung against the flanks of the Roman force while Hannibal's cavalry, led by his celebrated general Maharbal, crushed the Roman cavalry and light infantry deployed to protect the formation's flanks and rear and, in so doing, succeeded in encircling it completely. The Roman force now found itself unable to run or maneuver, completely surrounded by Hannibal's forces. It was one of the earliest examples of the pincer movement in the history of warfare.

The result was a massacre, one of the most vicious battles in the history of the world. Around 75% of the Roman army was cut down in the ensuing melee, which would be in the vicinity of between 50,000-80,000 soldiers depending on which initial estimates are considered to be accurate. Among the casualties was the luckless Consul Paullus, two-thirds of the city's Military Tribunes, a host of officials and noblemen from the most prominent Roman families, and almost a full third of the Senate. Hannibal's army killed so many prominent Romans that his men collected more than 200 gold signets from dead Romans, and he had the rings sent to Carthage to demonstrate his complete victory.

Livy described the scene, "So many thousands of Romans were dying ... Some, whom their wounds, pinched by the morning cold, had roused, as they were rising up, covered with blood, from the midst of the heaps of slain, were overpowered by the enemy. Some were found with their heads plunged into the earth, which they had excavated; having thus, as it appeared, made pits for themselves, and having suffocated themselves." If the casualty numbers are accurate, Hannibal's army slaughtered an average of 600 Roman soldiers every minute until nightfall ended the battle, and less than 15,000 Roman troops escaped, which required cutting their way through the center of Hannibal's army and fleeing to the nearby town of Canusium.

Cannae is still considered one of the greatest tactical victories in the history of warfare, and the fact the battle was a complete victory resulting in the wholesale annihilation of the enemy army made it the textbook example for military commanders to try to duplicate. Of course, others usually were unsuccessful. Cannae was the kind of complete victory that every commander from Caesar to Frederick the Great to Napoleon to Robert E. Lee sought, and that few generals save Caesar and Napoleon bagged whole armies is a testament to the near impossibility of achieving a victory like Cannae.

Not surprisingly, after the serious threat Hannibal posed during the Second Punic War, the Romans didn't wait much longer to take the fight to the Carthaginians in the Third Punic War, which ended with Roman legions smashing Carthage to rubble. As legend has it, the Romans literally salted the ground upon which Carthage stood to ensure its destruction once and for all. Despite having a major influence on the Mediterranean for nearly five centuries, little evidence of Carthage's past might survives. The city itself was reduced to nothing by the Romans, who sought to erase all physical evidence of its existence, and though its ruins have been excavated, they have not provided anywhere near the wealth of archaeological items or evidence as ancient locations like Rome, Athens, Syracuse, or even Troy.

The Battle of Cannae: The History of the Most Famous Battle of Ancient Rome's Most Decisive Military Defeat chronicles one of the most influential and decisive battles of antiquity. Along with pictures of important people, places, and events, you will learn about Cannae like never before.

The Battle of Cannae: The History and Legacy of Ancient Rome's Most Decisive Military
Defeat

About Charles River Editors

Introduction

Chapter 1: Prelude to the Second Punic War

Chapter 2: Hannibal's Invasion of Italy

Chapter 3: Opposing Forces

Chapter 4: Preparing the Trap at Cannae

Chapter 5: The Battle Plans

Chapter 6: The Battle of Cannae

Chapter ?: The Aftermath

Online Resources

Bibliography

Chapter 1: Prelude to the Second Punic War

Carthage's loss in the First Punic War resulted in a complete dearth of money and resources across their empire, which was a serious problem because Carthage relied chiefly on mercenary armies. Thousands of mercenaries throughout the Carthaginian Empire were suddenly not getting their wages, and the result was inevitable: war. An all-out insurrection of mercenary contingents throughout the Punic Empire, including Iberia, Sardinia and Corsica, and a renewed attack from the subjugated Lybian tribes, followed. Suddenly, Carthage was fighting for her very life, and grudgingly accepting military and financial aid from her two old enemies, Syracuse and Rome.

The war dragged on for two years, but by 238 Carthage was once again secure, with order restored to her dominions. Still, the cost had been heavy; taking advantage of Carthage's desperate situation, Rome had conveniently seized both Sardinia and Corsica, which had been plunged into lawlessness by the mercenary uprising, and there was nothing Carthage could do about it. The mines of Iberia, with their vast amounts of as yet untapped wealth, were still secure, but control of them was dubious.

Crisis, as so often occurs, had brought political change in its wake, and the Barcid family, led by Hamilcar Barca, had risen to prominence during the Mercenary Wars. Hamilcar was a skilled general who rapidly rose to command all of the Carthaginian armies by ousting the competition of his rival, Hanno the Great. Hamilcar was populist and had the support of the common people, whereas Hanno was a scion of the old Carthaginian aristocracy, but their power was on the wane. Thus, it was Hamilcar and his son-in-law, Hasdrubal the Fair, who subdued the Iberian cities, but the loyalty of these new dominions was far from certain. Rather than owing allegiance to Carthage, the Iberian cities looked to Hamilcar exclusively for guidance, making Spain a virtual Barcid fief.

Hamilcar was killed in battle in 228, so Hasdrubal took over as his successor and began to look for a way to strike back at Rome in retaliation for the First Punic War and the blatant land grab in the chaos that followed. It appears likely that around 225, Hasdrubal began plotting with the Gauls of the Po Valley in the north of Italy (the only as yet unconquered area in the Italian Peninsula) to launch an attack on Rome with Carthaginian backing, but the Senate got wind of the plan and ordered a pre-emptive strike of their own, leading to a five-year war which eventually led to the annexation of the Po Valley. Hasdrubal himself was assassinated in 221, possibly with Roman collusion.

Rather than solve the Romans' problem, Hasdrubal's death brought about the rise of the most famous Carthaginian of all. Hasdrubal was succeeded by his brother-in-law and Hamilcar's son, Hannibal. In the history of war, only a select few men always make the list of greatest generals, and one of them is Hannibal, who has the distinction of being the only man who nearly brought Rome to its knees before its decline almost 700 years after his time.

Hannibal. (Naepel, National Museum.)

A bust depicting Hannibal

For two years, Hannibal bided his time, consolidating his position in the Iberian peninsula and massing his forces, abiding by one of the greatest military truths and one which doubtless his tutors and his father, with their tales of Alexander and Alcibiades, had contributed to instill in him: numbers do not matter so much as concentration of force, i.e. what troops are available to fight in one single critical location, at any given time. Meanwhile, even as Hannibal was preparing to strike out against their very heart, the Romans seem to have grown unusually complacent; after all, Hannibal was new to overall command, and with both Hamilcar and Hasdrubal dead, they must have felt themselves secure. When in 218 Hannibal resurrected his brother-in-law's plan for a joint Gaulish and Carthaginian invasion of the Italian peninsula, the Romans were caught napping, something which they would live to regret in the following years.

Hannibal needed a *casus belli*, and in 219 BCE the Romans obliged him with one by forming an alliance with the powerful Iberian city of Saguntum, well south of the line drawn along the Ebro, and unilaterally declaring it a Roman protectorate. Hannibal took this for outright rebellion, and acted accordingly, investing the city and besieging it for eight months until it fell. He then protested to Carthage that Rome had broken the terms of their agreement with them, declaring that there could be only one feasible course of action: war. The Carthaginian rulers, having been burned once before, were wary of becoming embroiled in a new conflict with Rome, but such was Hannibal's popularity with the troops in the Iberian peninsula that, with the memory of the Mercenary Wars still fresh in their minds, they acceded to his demands rather than risk a full-blown mutiny.

Chapter 2: Hannibal's Invasion of Italy

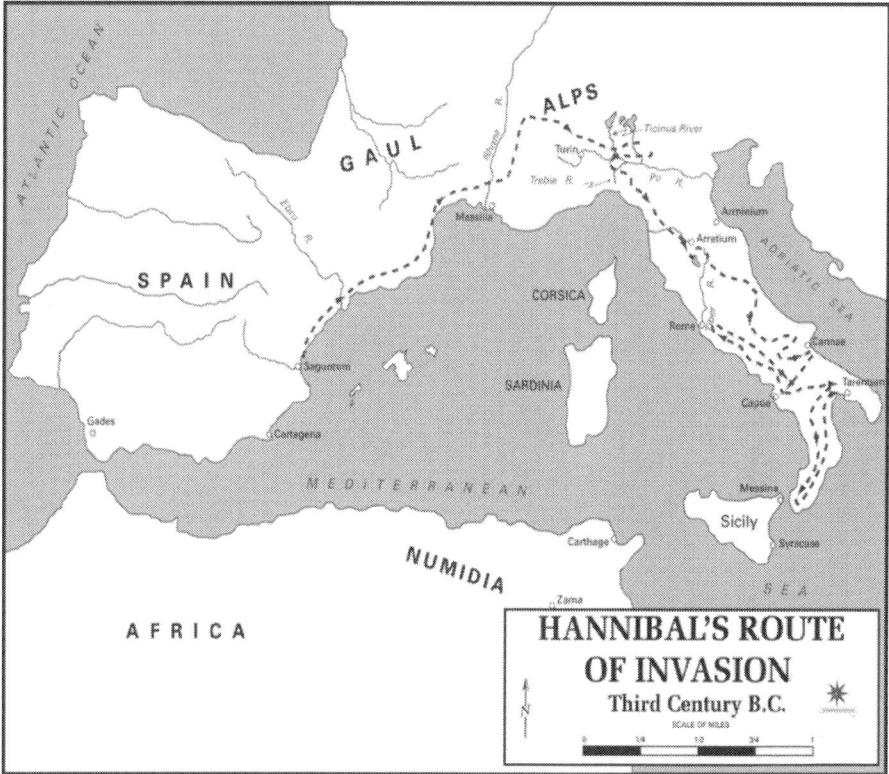

HANNIBAL'S ROUTE
OF INVASION
Third Century B.C.

Estimated march of Hannibal's Invasion of Italy by the United States Military Academy

In the spring of 218 BCE, at the head of approximately 50,000 infantry, 15,000 cavalry, and 50 war elephants, Hannibal began marching northeast. His plan was breathtakingly ambitious; he would march through the Pyrenees, across southern Gaul, over the Alps and into Italy proper, thereby avoiding the heavily fortified border in the northwest of Italy. It was a route no general had ever taken before, let alone a general with so many animals (including elephants). His father Hamilcar had been defeated trying to invade southern Italy and attempting to outfight the Roman navy at sea; Hannibal would not make the same mistake.

Pushing aside with contemptuous ease the stiff resistance of the Pyrenean tribes, who contested every step of the way from their strongholds of the mountain passes, Hannibal pushed forwards with remarkable speed, leaving behind a detachment of some 10,000 Iberian soldiers to keep his lines of communication open and pacify the tumultuous region. He then marched on into southern Gaul, negotiating with the local chieftains and outfighting those who had a mind to contest his advance. His speed of maneuver, and his ability to move his army across rough terrain, proved unmatched in the ancient world since the time of Alexander the Great. By that point, his army, which now numbered some 40,000 infantry, 8,000 cavalry, and around 40 war elephants, danced up the valley of the Rhone to evade a Roman force sent to bar his passage southwards through the strategically vital gap in the mountains where the Alps meet the Mediterranean. With that route closed to him, Hannibal, undaunted, struck south and east across the Alps themselves.

Exactly what route he took is still the subject of hotly contested debate today, and even Roman scholars writing shortly after his prodigious feat seem to have no clear idea of where precisely he made his passage, but one thing is certain: it was one of the most remarkable maneuvers in military history. There were no roads greater than a goat-track across the Alps, none of them continuous, and the high passes were smothered by snow, often year-round, with drifts dozens of feet deep. Moreover, those passes included other hazards, such as potential rockfalls, and the barren terrain offered limited supplies. To top it all off, these passes were crawling with bellicose tribesmen who lived by banditry and hid in impregnable fortresses perched atop sheer crags. To Hannibal's army, most of them Iberians from the sun-baked plains of southern Spain or Carthaginians from the hot deserts of Northern Africa, the Alps must have looked like an icy Hell.

Hannibal's passage of the Alps remains the most famous event of his life and legend, and even though the location of his crossing matters little compared to the fact that he ultimately did get across, it has nonetheless been the most compelling mystery of his life for over 2,000 years. Even ancient historians were intrigued and tried to figure out the answer. The well known ancient Greek historian Polybius mentioned that Hannibal's men came into conflict with a Celtic tribe, the Allobroges, which was situated near the northern part of the range along the banks of the river Isère. The famous Roman historian Livy, writing over 150 years after Polybius, claimed Hannibal took a southerly route.

It is believed that both historians used the same source, a soldier in Hannibal's army, Sosylus of Lacedaemon, who wrote a history of the Second Punic War. Geographers and historians have pointed to the 6 most likely mountain passes that could have actually been used and then tried to narrow it down by finding one that seems to match the descriptions of both Livy and Polybius. A handful of historians used those accounts to theorize that Hannibal crossed the Alps at the Col du Montgenèvre pass, which would have been in the southern part of the range near northwest Italy. That also happened to be one of the better known road passes in the ancient world, and it was used often for diplomacy.

Wherever the crossing, and despite the innumerable difficulties, Hannibal got across. He reached the rolling foothills of Northern Italy several months later, at the head of 20,000 infantry, 4,000 cavalry, and a mere handful of war elephants (the great beasts having fared none too well, as was to be expected, in the mountain passes). If figures relating to his troop numbers before and after his celebrated crossing are to be believed, only half of the men Hannibal marched into the Alps marched back out again, and Hannibal must have known that no supply convoys could ever hope to cross where his army had passed. Nor, with the Roman navy's supremacy in the Mediterranean, could he have much hope of resupply or retreat by sea. Like Caesar would do nearly 170 years later crossing the Rubicon, Hannibal had cast the die. He and his men were left with no choice but victory or death.

Costly as it was, Hannibal's choice to cross the Alps was not done so for vainglorious reasons. By appearing suddenly in Northern Italy, crossing terrain that was reckoned to be impassable, Hannibal took the Romans completely by surprise, and the main Roman army that had been mobilized to fight Hannibal was caught completely wrong-footed. When news of Hannibal's appearance reached its commander, Publius Scipio (father of the redoubtable Scipio Africanus, who would cross swords with Hannibal himself in the years to come), he was in the process of pushing his men across the Pyrenees and into Iberia. He quickly loaded his rearguard onto ships, sailed across to Italy, and hurried to intercept Hannibal by forced march.

Scipio engaged Hannibal's forces at Ticinus, but he could only hope to fight a delaying action with the limited troops at his disposal. Hannibal's celebrated Numidian cavalry routed Scipio's forces, and would have killed Scipio himself had it not been for Scipio Africanus' timely rescue. Emboldened by this Roman defeat, the Gauls of the Po valley rose in revolt, sending a large force (around 20,000 men) to join Hannibal's army. Hannibal then marched his force south of Scipio's main base at Placentia, on the Trebia river, cutting him off from the support of Consul Sempronius Longus, who was marching up from southern Italy to come to his aid and bring Hannibal to battle. However, when the provisions promised to his army by the Cisalpine Gauls failed to materialize, Hannibal was forced to abandon his tactically superior position to capture the supply depots at Clastidium, allowing Longus and Scipio to join their forces near the Trebia.

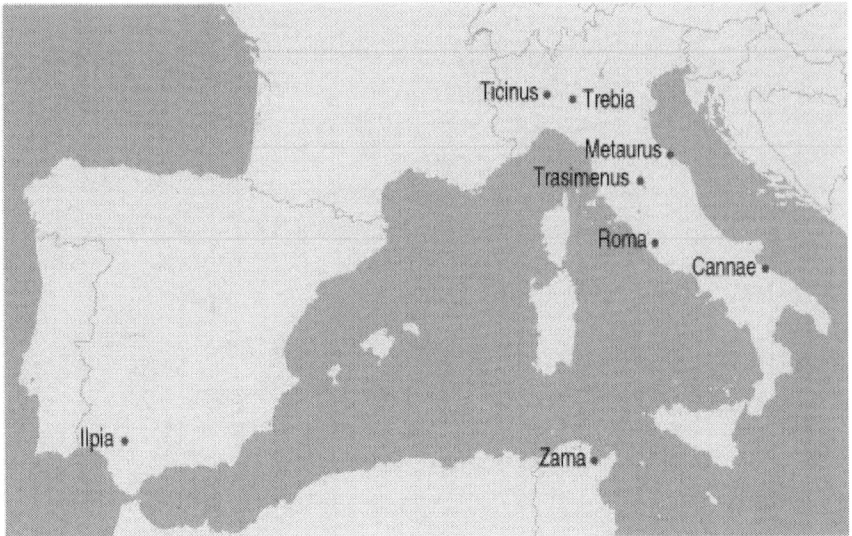

Although the Roman Senate was now hurriedly raising legions in Rome, and two powerful Roman armies had joined together, Hannibal apparently remained unfazed. He promptly marched on the Roman camp on the Trebia, making a show of force and inviting Scipio and Longus to attack him. The two Roman generals obliged, throwing their celebrated infantry across the Trebia in order to attack Hannibal's forces, arrayed on the bluffs above the river. Exhausted by their river crossing, the Roman troops became entangled in a bloody melee with Hannibal's infantry, fighting each other to a standstill until Hannibal unveiled his master stroke. Concealed from the Roman infantry by the terrain until the last moment, his light infantry and cavalry stormed into the Roman flanks, enveloped the entire force and, trapping the legions with their backs to the river, annihilated them. It was a crushing victory for Hannibal, and a disaster for Rome. It would be the first of many.

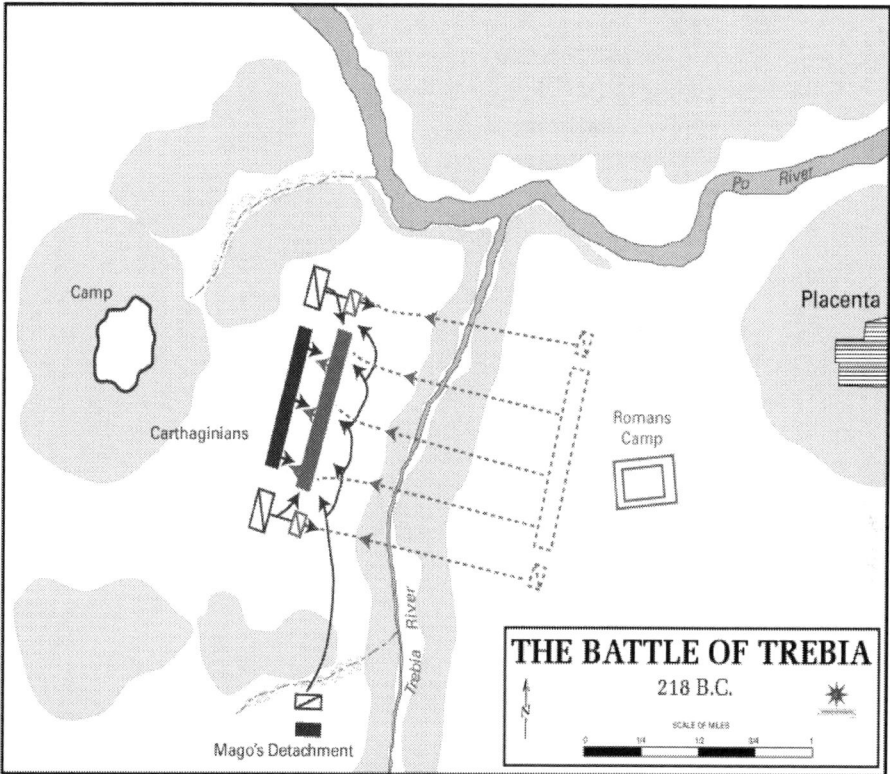

THE BATTLE OF TREBIA

218 B.C.

SCALE OF MILES

0   1/4   1/2   3/4   1

Camp

Placenta

Po River

Carthaginians

Romans Camp

Trebia River

Mago's Detachment

By this point, the campaigning season, which traditionally stopped during the winter months, was virtually over. Hannibal decided to winter his troops in Cisalpine Gaul, but he quickly wore out his welcome there. Possibly because the Gauls were displeased at how Hannibal had used their levies to grind down the Roman forces, the supplies they provided were stilted and ungenerous. In early spring, Hannibal decided to find himself a more secure base and made ready to carry the war into Italy proper. However, despite the winter lull, the Romans had not been idle. Two consular armies, under consuls Servilius and Flaminius, had marched at the beginning of the new year to block Hannibal's routes to the south and east, fortifying their positions there and effectively immuring him within northern Italy. A normal general would have thought himself trapped. Hannibal, however, had a plan. To the south lay the Apennines Mountains and the huge swampy delta of the Arno river, in modern Tuscany, an area reckoned impassable by any army.

Hannibal must have reckoned that after what he had faced in the Alps, he and his men were ready for any challenge. After a brief pause for consideration, he ordered his army to march for the Arno. The Apennines were less of a challenge than the Alps had been, and Hannibal's forces made decent enough time as they crossed through them, but Hannibal himself suffered a debilitating injury, losing an eye to a virulent infection (believed to be conjunctivitis) that kept him bedridden for a spell. His army then descended into the basin of the Arno, but the going was far harder than even Hannibal could have anticipated. The entire region was a festering swamp, with not a single scrap of dry, solid land for his men and horses to sleep on. Hannibal quickly realized he had marched his men into a death-trap. With no choice but to push on, he and his men marched uninterruptedly for four days and three nights, in water and mud that often came up to their waists, with no rest except what they could snatch on their feet. Hundreds, perhaps thousands of Hannibal's men perished on the march. Some were drowned, others were swallowed by quicksand, others contracted malaria or dysentery from drinking the swampy water, and still more simply died of exhaustion. By the end of the march, Hannibal had lost the last of his war elephants, as well as virtually all of his supplies and wheeled transport, but he was now in Etruria, Roman heartland, with both Flaminius and Servilius to the north of him.

As Polybius noted in his account, Hannibal had reached an important crossroad in his campaign. As Polybius wrote, "[Hannibal] calculated that, if he passed the camp and made a descent into the district beyond, Flaminius (partly for fear of popular reproach and partly of personal irritation) would be unable to endure watching passively the devastation of the country but would spontaneously follow him…and give him opportunities for attack." Hannibal needed to bring Flaminius to battle, to avoid the danger of having a large enemy force to his rear, but he found Flaminius too passive to give him the battle he sought.

In order to persuade the Consul – who had a healthy fear of his abilities – to take to the field against him, Hannibal set about ravaging the surrounding Etrurian countryside, sacking towns, burning markets and generally wreaking havoc in the hope that Flaminius would become so incensed that he would be forced to defend the Italian heartland, or that a direct order should arrive from Rome ordering him to do so. Hannibal, though his military strategy was sound, was not as strong in his political choices as he was in battle: by devastating Etruria, he lost support among the local people, whom he might otherwise have been able to lure away from their alliance to Rome. Moreover, despite Hannibal's best efforts, Flaminius stubbornly stayed put in his defensive position. Frustrated by the Roman general's supineness, Hannibal marched around Flaminius's flank and cut him off from Rome, the kind of turning movement in warfare that was rarely used in the ancient world but became standard fare (and often the ultimate strategic goal) over the next 2,000 years. Even with such a massive threat to his lines of supply and communication, Flaminius still refused to march, so Hannibal turned and marched southwards. This time, with the Senate demanding what exactly he was playing at, Flaminius had no choice but to chase him.

Flaminius marched his 30,000 men after Hannibal, but the Carthaginian forces outstripped him. Desperate to bring the enemy to battle, Flaminius pushed recklessly onwards without scouting his line of advance, a mistake which was to cost him dear. On the northern edge of Lake Trasimene, Flaminius marched his army through a narrow defile and onto a small plain that was ringed by wooded mountains, through which his trackers reported Hannibal had marched some time previously. It was only when the last of the Roman forces had marched through the defile that Hannibal swung the jaws of his trap shut: his cavalry rushed forward from concealed positions to close the only gap through which Flaminius's force could retreat, and then his entire army poured howling out of the woods and fell onto the Romans before they had the chance to take up battle positions. In the ensuing desperate melee, virtually the entire Roman army was wiped out: 15,000 or more, including Flaminius himself, were killed, cut down in the melee or drowned in the lake trying to swim to safety. Around 5,000 more Roman soldiers were captured, and the remainder scattered into the hills. In one masterful stroke, Hannibal had disposed of the last field army in Northern Italy, successfully executing antiquity's greatest ambush. Rome herself was now at his mercy.

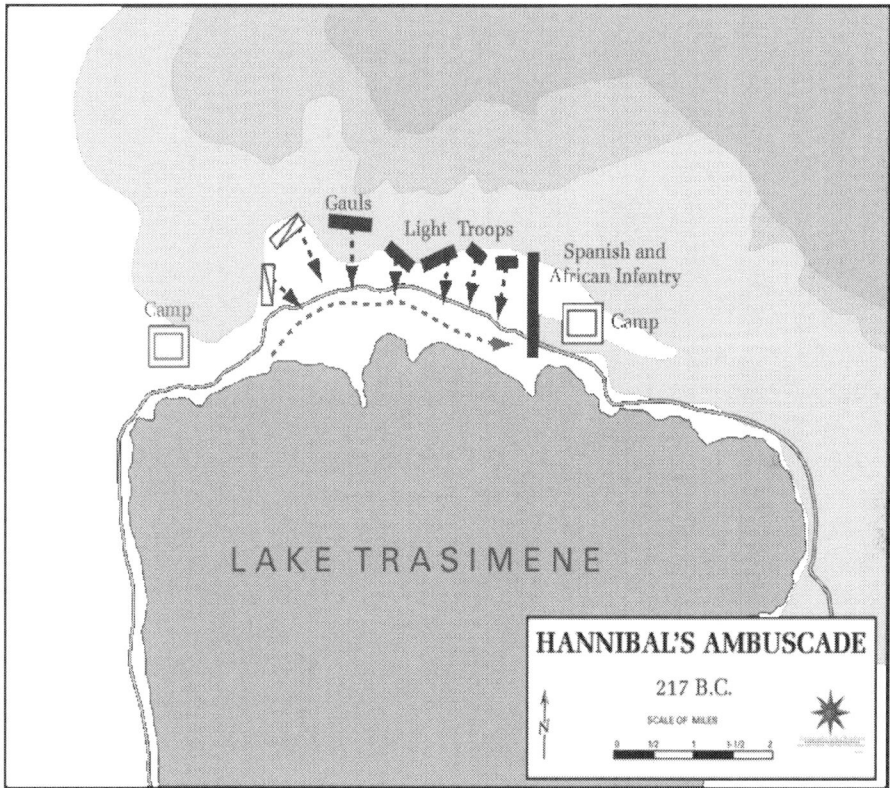

Hannibal was now in an ideal position to strike at Rome, but he chose not to do so. If he ever had any siege artillery in his baggage train (no mention is made of it in the original sources) then he lost it in the Alps or in the swamps of the Arno, because he had none available to invest Rome, nor, apparently, the engineering expertise either among his Carthaginian troops or his Gaulish levies to manufacture any. Without siege engines, he could still have chosen to ring the city with earthworks and lay siege to it, but instead he decided to march into Southern Italy, where he hoped to incite revolt among Rome's subject states.

Statue of Fabius Maximus

The Romans, desperate for something, anything, to rid themselves of this Carthaginian nemesis, appointed General Fabius Maximus as Dictator, an extraordinary measure which was only undertaken in times of the greatest crisis. Maximus, who had a healthy respect for Hannibal's generalship and was painfully aware of what had befallen Roman armies in pitched battles against him, now developed the "Fabian Strategy", which focused on indirect, attritional warfare. This strategy called for relying on skirmishes, ambushes, and dilatory tactics to harass, undermine and frighten Hannibal's forces, avoiding pitched battle which would almost certainly have proven ruinous. Though Maximus' tactics were effective, this indirect mode of warfare was considered dishonorable, even cowardly, by many Romans, who derisively nicknamed him "Cunctator" ("The Delayer").

Frustrated by Maximus' tactics, Hannibal took out his spite by ravaging the country estates and cities of the Apulian region before making his way into Campania, one of the most important agrarian regions in Italy because of its vast fertile plains that produced harvests crucial to feeding the great masses of Rome. Even the threat to the Campanian exports failed to draw Maximus into open battle, but Hannibal was so overzealous in his harrowing of Campania that, he soon realized, come the winter his army would have nothing to live off. Accordingly, he decided to march back to Apulia, but found his path blocked by a number of different Roman contingents that Maximus had placed at crucial passes to bar his way back. Hannibal responded with customary brilliance, by feinting his entire army at a thickly wooded hill, suggesting he was going to march through the forest and ignore the pass, and when the Roman army repositioned to attempt to bar his way, promptly marched his men about and through the pass they had so obligingly left unguarded, a tactical master-stroke which so damaged Maximus' already tarnished reputation as a commander that he was forced to step down as Dictator. As British historian Adrian Goldsworthy noted, the maneuver was "a classic of ancient generalship, finding its way into nearly every historical narrative of the war and being used by later military manuals".

Chapter 3: Opposing Forces

Fabius Maximus was quite content with striking at Hannibal's army and its few lines of logistical support with small raiding forces. In this way, he could keep Hannibal's thinly stretched out support lines under constant tension and nervous. Maximus' countrymen, however, disagreed with his careful and length approach to the Carthaginian problem. The Roman Republic wanted a Roman army to meet Hannibal's army on the field of battle, the people of Rome wanted that Roman army to drive Hannibal from the Italian Peninsula. The Roman people were still angry over the defeats that their armies had suffered at the battle of Trebia and the battle of Lake Trasimene. The Roman Republic wanted to avenge those dead legions and the only way in which that could be done, they believed, was through strength of arms and not through cunning or being skilled in the art of deception.

In addition to the sting of not one but two severe losses, the Roman people were also upset about the fact that Hannibal and his troops were marching at will through the peninsula. Fabius Maximus, it seemed to the people, was allowing Hannibal time to gather his far-flung troops. This gathering of soldiers would create an even larger Carthaginian army, which in turn would require an even greater number of Roman and allied troops to beat him. And finally, like so many other people throughout history, the Roman people wanted a quick victory. They had no desire to witness – or to be held hostage by – a long and protracted campaign which would give them nothing but small victories.

The people of Rome didn't want to see a hungry Hannibal Barca slipping away from the grip of Roman justice; they wanted to see the bulk of Hannibal's army dead upon the field of battle, with the others running for their lives or prisoners in the hands of the Roman legions. They wanted the backbone of the Carthaginian army broken, and they wanted Hannibal himself to be marched through the streets of Rome in chains, part of a Roman general's triumphant return to the city.

Having fallen out of favor with both the Roman people and the Roman government, Fabius Maximus found that his services as dictator were no longer needed. Instead, the Roman government set up the tried and true process of electing officials who would, in their capacities as Roman generals, bring the war to Hannibal Barca and attempt to remove him from the Italian Peninsula. The Roman Republic had certain unique cultural and societal requirements placed upon any male citizen who sought to move upwards in society or have a successful career in politics. The most important of these requirements, and the one which could not be avoided, was for that individual to have served for at least some period of time in the military. Thus, no Roman citizen who had any sort of political aspirations could honestly expect to be able to achieve his goals if he did not spend a minimum of at least two years in the service of a legion. That way, when it came time for the elected officials of Rome to take the command of a legion, the politicians in question had at least a rudimentary understanding of military matters, engineering, logistics, and tactics.

Following the destruction of the Roman legions at the Battle of Trebia and the Battle of Lake Trasimene, Rome spent significant time and resources raising new legions to replace those that were lost. The Roman government was confident that the Republic could levy new legions from within the borders of the Italian Peninsula, and the creation of new legions, which was to be done solely from Romans and Rome's Italian allies, showed Hannibal exactly what the Roman government thought of him. The Romans knew Hannibal and his Carthaginians and his army could fight, but they had no intent of interrupting campaigns being carried out in other provinces or territories.

While various legion commanders out in the far-flung reaches of the growing Roman Republic offered to return to hunt down and drive out Hannibal and his army, the Roman government told these generals to focus solely upon the campaigns that their legions were actively engaged in. In other words, the citizens back in Rome would settle the problem of Hannibal Barca themselves.

Of course, since Rome was intent on having their existing legions continue to wage wars in other provinces and territories, new legions had to be formed, and this required several steps. Gathering new recruits wasn't difficult since service in the military was a requirement for social advancement, but the new soldiers had to be trained to fight as heavy infantry and work together. For these men to be trained properly, however, they needed to have equipment, including swords, shields, javelins, helmets and assorted armor. In addition to this, the new recruits had to be clothed, fed and paid. Finally, commanders for the newly established legions were going to have to be found.

The senators of Rome clamored to be given the right to command cohorts within the new legions, but the right to command the legions themselves would fall upon the shoulders of former consuls, and overall command of the massive army that was being created would be given to the two current consuls.

With the abandonment of Fabius Maximus' strategic plan to starve Hannibal and his force off of the Italian Peninsula by striking at the few supply lines that the Carthaginian general had, and also by denying him the ability to live off of the land, the Roman government devised a new battle plan. This plan was extremely simple and direct, and it spoke quite frankly to the Roman desire to resolve the current conflict with Carthage through strength of arms. The Roman Republic and her allies on the Italian Peninsula would gather an army together that would dwarf Hannibal's force.

The rationale behind this strategy was that if Hannibal could defeat Roman forces that were of an equal size, or one which was slightly larger, then surely if the Romans had numbers on their side they would be victorious. The Romans understandably believed that the tactical abilities of Hannibal and the skills of his veteran troops could be negated by an overwhelmingly superior force of trained legionaries; after all, it's not as though the Romans didn't know how to fight.

With that, the Roman Republic and her Italian allies – the Etruscans and the Samnites – set about the long process of building a grand army. By using those few veterans who had survived the battles of both Trebia and Lake Trasimene as core elements, and also by using a training program that had served the legions well for decades, the Romans and their allies were able to build entirely new legions in order to fight Hannibal and the Carthaginian army. The Etruscans and the Samnites, who modeled their own legions upon those of Rome's, set about the task of building and preparing their own new legions as well.

In a relatively short amount of time, the Roman Republic, with her allies beside her, had assembled the largest army that they had ever put into the field. While there are, of course, widely varying accounts and estimates as to the actual size of the Roman and allied combined force, most historians believe Polybius' account, which claimed the forces reached a combined total of an estimated 86,000 troops. Rome, of course, brought with her the lion's share of the men with a full 8 legions, each legion at full strength with 5,000 men per legion. In addition to this, the Roman legions were accompanied by an estimated 2,000 of their own Roman cavalry. The Etruscans and the Samnites combined to create a total of 8 legions as well, as well as an additional 4,000 cavalry.

Since this new Roman army was essentially the combination of two separate armies, both of the Roman consuls were in joint command of the new army. This was in stark contrast to the usual system, which dictated that only one consul retained control of the entire force. In this case, both consuls, being equals in the Roman government, would share the responsibilities of commanding such a tremendous force, and when the army was in the field, the two consuls would alternate days on which they commanded.

The two consuls who commanded this newly formed Roman army were Lucius Aemilius Paullus and Gaius Terentius Varro. Varro would be the scapegoat for the Roman massacre at Cannae for over two millennia, though this stigma is not due to anything he did or failed to do at the battle. Instead, the fact the blame was laid at the feet of Varro is a result of two specific factors. The first was that Varro had the "bad luck" of surviving the massacre at Cannae; in accordance with Roman expectations, Rome would have fully have supported any decision he made that resulted in suicide. The second significant factor was Varro's actual position in Roman society, notably the fact that his family was not well to do. While his family was of an aristocratic line, they lacked the financial ability to defend Varro's name and character following the battle.

This was not the case for Lucius Aemilius Paullus' family, and Paullus died while attempting to escape the massive trap devised by Hannibal at Cannae. Since Paullus' family was significantly wealthy, they were able to set the blame for the Roman defeat squarely upon the shoulders upon Varro, and his descendants were able to conduct a successful propaganda campaign over the centuries. The family consistently painted Varro as a rash coward and a fool, and they also called into question his military abilities. Implicit in the criticism was Varro's low place on the aristocratic social scale. Paullus, on the other hand, was portrayed as an ideal Roman citizen who did his duty and was betrayed by the ineptitude of a colleague. Furthermore, the Paullus family had great assistance in their efforts to demonize Varro because the ancient historian Polybius owed a great deal to his patron, Lucius Aemilius Paullus' grandfather.

Of course, all that was in the future. The Roman generals alternated the command of the combined force from day to day, and they had a vastly different tactical approach to the situations that they came upon. Paullus has been described as a man who was the most conservative of the two consuls, one who chose his actions carefully and thus planned accordingly for any engagement. Varro, however, has been described as a man who was both reckless and heedless of danger, and unheeding of advice offered to him. According to Polybius and other contemporaries, Varro ignored advice offered up by Paullus on the day of the battle, August 2, 216 BCE. They claimed Paullus cautioned Varro against marching the army out to meet Hannibal and the Carthaginian army at Cannae.

Unlike the massive army the Roman Republic and her allies had assembled and were marching through Italy looking for Hannibal, the Carthaginian army was not a homogeneous force. Carthage had relied upon naval power to make its fortune and spread its power and position throughout the Mediterranean, and in order for Carthage to continue to do these things, and in order for the merchants to continue turning a profit, the city elders had hired mercenaries when fighting on land was necessary. The hiring of mercenary forces for land battles also had a tremendous impact on the Carthaginian navy; while a small unit of Carthaginian men would also be part of the army, the ships of the Carthaginian navy were manned by Carthaginian sailors. These ships, in turn, would then be used to transport the mercenaries whom the city had hired to the necessary battlefields.

Throughout most of its history, the armies Carthage sent to the field were commanded by Carthaginians who had served in the infantry and cavalry. The one exception shortly before the Second Punic War had occurred during the First Punic War when Carthage had hired a Spartan general to drive the Romans away from Carthage.

While the army itself was commanded by a Carthaginian, the mercenary units making up the bulk of the army were commanded and officered by their own men. Thus, the Numidian cavalry would have a Numidian officer commanding them, and a Gallic infantry unit would have their own Gallic commander. It was the responsibility of the Carthaginian general to ensure that all of the various units of the army were able to function together as a single entity.

Some Carthaginian generals carried out this task better than others, of course, but none were as skilled or successful as Hannibal. One of the ways which Hannibal used his charisma was to combine it with other aspects of his personality, such as his personal bravery. Hannibal could often be found fighting beside his men in the thick of a battle, leading them from the front and by his own example. He harbored no fear of death and trusted in the strength and battle prowess of the men under his command. His willingness to place his own fate into their hands made them admire him, and in turn they were inspired by him.

At the same time, the mercenary army Hannibal had helped to create and which he commanded was possibly the finest army the city of Carthage had ever put into the field. Like all of the Carthaginian armies prior to the Second Punic War, Hannibal's force was an amalgamation of mercenary units, and these individual units operated as part of the whole. They had been chosen from countries that were either strictly mercenary in their dealing with the Roman Republic, or they consisted of people who had no love for the Romans. The various mercenary units which made up Hannibal's army had also been chosen for their specialties, such as cavalry, light infantry, heavy infantry, and spearmen. Some of the units, such as the Numidians, fought strictly for coin and out of no particular animosity towards the Roman Republic. The Gallic forces, however, had been fighting on and off with the Roman Republic for nearly two centuries prior to the battle of Cannae.

Thus it was that the force Hannibal Barca commanded at Cannae had a vast array of mercenaries, consisting of Spanish, Gallic, Libyans, Iberians, Numidians and small units of professional Carthaginian soldiers.

The Numidians excelled in the art of war from horseback and were frighteningly skillful cavalrymen. The ancient historians recorded that the Numidians rode from their earliest youth and that they had the disturbing ability to throw a spear effectively from the back of a galloping horse.

The Libyans that fought for Hannibal did so as heavy infantry at the battle, and these Libyans were equipped with the armor and weapons of Roman legionaries who had been killed in previous engagements with Hannibal's army. With this armor, as well as their own short spears and captured Roman short swords, the Libyans fought in a phalanx formation. This particular formation had served the Libyans well when battling Macedonian units, and it would serve them well again as they fought against the densely packed formation of the Roman legions.

The Spanish and Gallic forces Hannibal had hired and integrated into the Carthaginian army were not nearly as disciplined or organized. These two particular groups were wild and could not be counted upon in difficult situations, and their specific fighting style had them trained to withdraw when too much pressure was placed upon them. However, the fact they couldn't stand up against the Romans on open ground also meant Hannibal knew how to utilize them. Indeed, he made certain that he would remain with the Spanish and Gallic troops when his trap was sprung upon the Roman army marching towards him.

Chapter 4: Preparing the Trap at Cannae

Hannibal understood the temperament of the Roman people and the Roman Republic itself, and he was also well aware that the tremendous size of the army the Romans and their allies had assembled meant that the Romans were anxious to finish the war. Thus, he could rightly assume the Roman commanders would be seeking a single decisive battle.

Armed with this knowledge, as well as with his intimate knowledge of the tactics of the Roman legions, Hannibal balanced the weight of his knowledge against what he knew of his own army. Most of the forces under his command were exceptionally skilled veterans, and they had survived the deadly march through the Pyrenees and over the Alps. In addition to their combat skills and their abilities as soldiers, the men of the Carthaginian army were fiercely loyal to Hannibal.

As such, Hannibal prepared a trap which he believed the Romans would march into. The maneuver would be simple, but it would also be done on a massive scale. He would use a double enveloping move with his forces, which would not require any sort of trickery or a grand ruse but tight coordination on both wings of the Carthaginian army. Hannibal's job would be made easier by the Romans' impatience and desire to win a decisive victory, which ensured they would push forward and put in all their men.

Planning for the battle to come, and with the Romans refusing to fight on the first day – as Hannibal had known they would since Lucius Aemilius Paullus had been in command on that day – Hannibal was able to select the field of battle at Cannae. The battlefield of Cannae is located in the southeastern portion of the Italian Peninsula, and the Aufidus River serves as both a barrier and the border of the battlefield. When Hannibal originally chose Cannae and marched his army into it, he did so for three specific reasons. The first reason was that Cannae was equipped with a large storehouse, which contained a vast amount of supplies that would serve his army. The constant lack of logistical support from Carthage and a continuous lack of necessary supplies made Cannae an excellent choice for resupply. The second reason was the land itself; by seizing Cannae, Hannibal gained not only the supplies but also a commanding position of a large area. This commanding position would enable him to strike out against a large array of

Roman and allied targets, and the Carthaginians would have exceptional mobility at Cannae, allowing Hannibal to use cavalry raids against Roman foragers and water gatherers. The third and final reason that Hannibal seized the area of Cannae was because he could count on a strong Roman response. Hannibal knew the Romans would react as quickly as possible because there was a large amount of supplies at Cannae and the position granted the Carthaginians access to large swaths of Roman territory. Hannibal rightly figured his position at Cannae would be far too much for Lucius Aemilius Paullus and Gaius Terentius Varro to ignore.

Sure enough, the two consuls rapidly marched the army to Cannae, and within two days' march, Varro and Paullus discovered Hannibal's army camped on the left side of the Aufidus River. With this discovery, the Roman generals made the decision to encamp as well.

Unlike Hannibal's camp, however, the Roman encampment consisted of two separate sites. The first and larger of the two camps was also pitched upon the left side of the Aufidus, just 6 miles away from the Carthaginian camp. Both Varro and Paullus were in the larger camp since the majority of the Roman and allied forces were established there, while the second and smaller of the two camps (which consisted of an estimated 10,000 troops) was established to ensure the protection of the foraging and water bearing parties sent forth from the main camp. These supply parties would need to provide sufficient water for nearly 80,000 men. In addition to protecting these important supply parties, the legionaries in the smaller camp were also supposed to harass any supply parties that might issue forth from the Carthaginian camp.

By this time, Hannibal had plenty of experience operating within the dangerous confines of an enemy country. Knowing full well that his own supply parties would need protection, and that the Roman supply parties would need the same, Hannibal took appropriate steps to protect his own while destroying the enemy's. Varro and Paullus dispatched small cavalry and infantry units to carry out the necessary tasks of protection and harassment, but Hannibal dispatched elements of his superior cavalry to disrupt the Romans. Thanks to these efforts, the Roman foragers and water bearers could not bring enough supplies and water into the rest of the Roman army. This lack of water would prove to be a factor in the massacre that followed.

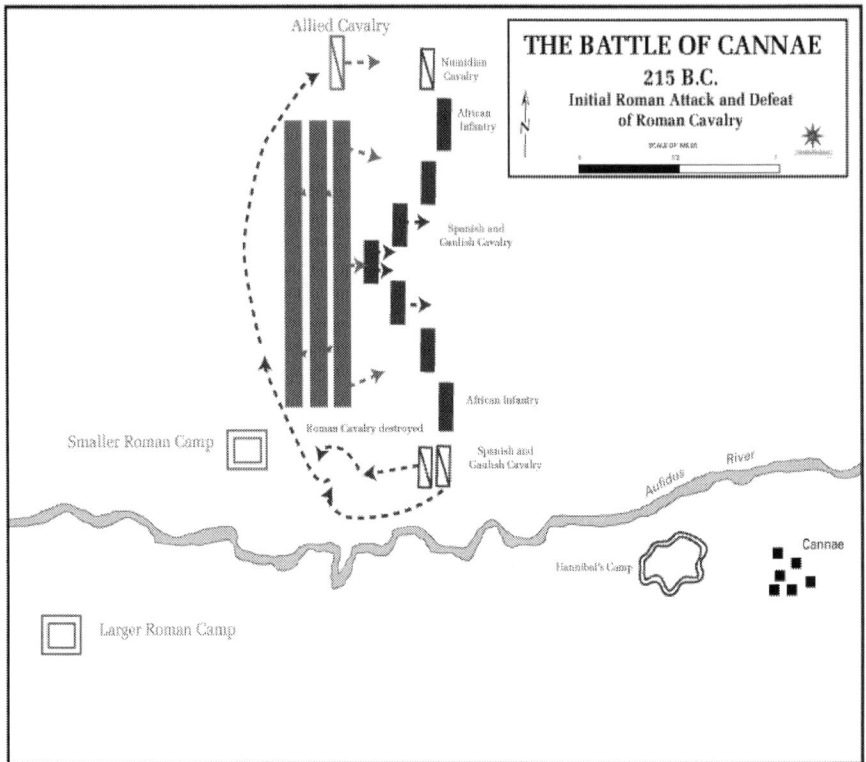

A map of the initial dispositions at Cannae

On August 1, 216 BCE, acting on information about the Roman army, Hannibal rode out and offered battle to the Romans. He did this because the information indicated Paullus was in command of the army that day. Hannibal judged that Paullus would not want to engage immediately in battle, and he was right, as Paullus refused to take the field. Paullus wanted to avoid fighting Hannibal in open ground, despite the significant advantage in manpower.

While that may have been wise, Hannibal knew that the consuls were alternating command of the Roman army and that he would be facing Varro on the following day. He also knew that Varro, unlike Paullus, tended to be both rash and impulsive, and he counted upon the Roman commander's infamous impatience. Hannibal also assumed Paullus' refusal to fight would make Varro even more impatient to fight on August 2.

Chapter 5: The Battle Plans

On the morning of the battle, Varro believed he had managed to pin down Hannibal and the Carthaginian army in one place, and with the Carthaginians at Cannae, the Roman army would finally be able to bring Hannibal and his army to the decisive battle that all of Rome was seeking. Indeed, it appeared to the Romans that the Carthaginian general had finally trapped himself. The Roman force was nearly twice the size of the Carthaginians, and the battlefield had a wide plain which could ensure not only that the Romans could put their entire force in the field but that Hannibal couldn't hide any reserves. The Romans were painfully aware that Hannibal had used subterfuge to bring about reserves at critical junctures and surprise his opponents.

Perhaps most crucially, Varro thought Hannibal made a critical error by positioning his army with its back to the Aufidus River. The Aufidus River ran along the rear of the Carthaginian army and along its left flank as well, so Varro believed that it would prevent the Carthaginians from running when pressed. Combined with his numerical advantage, the Carthaginians would be unable to cut their way out to escape as well, and the right flank itself would be closed off as a route of escape for the Carthaginians by the presence of Roman cavalry.

At the Battle of Trebia, the Roman infantry had succeeded in breaking through the center of the Carthaginian infantry, but Hannibal had hidden Carthaginian troops as reinforcements. The Roman general hoped, then, to recreate this breaking of the Carthaginian infantry at the battle of Cannae. Varro sought, however, to do it on a much larger scale than had been done at Trebia by increasing the depth of his infantry and stacking it. This meant that rather than spreading his tens of thousands of infantry out on a wide front that might push the Carthaginian army back into the Aufidus River, Varro wished solely to break the Carthaginian line. He would do this to show the strength of Rome's legions and for the psychological effect it would have upon the Carthaginian army forced to watch as Varro split the line in two. With the army thus separated, the Roman and allied infantry would crush the Carthaginians, destroying the various mercenary units piecemeal.

The Roman cavalry, which Varro would deploy on his own flanks, were to destroy the Carthaginian cavalry. Through the destruction of the Carthaginian cavalry, and by driving those that survived back into the flanks of the Carthaginian infantry, Varro would have the remnants of the Carthaginian cavalry and infantry trapped.

Once the Carthaginian army was separated, Varro would have the Roman infantry attack the right flank and center of the Carthaginians on the left (in an attempt to outflank them). The Roman cavalry, in turn, would then be used to attack that section's left flank. For the right section of the divided Carthaginian army, the opposite would be true; the Roman infantry would thus be on the Carthaginians' left and center, with the right flank of that section being hemmed in by the Roman cavalry. The Aufidus River would run behind both segments of the Carthaginian army, forming a final wall which the Carthaginians would not be able to breach without a great loss of life.

To Varro, the fears of his co-commander were unfounded. By the end of the day, Varro was certain that the Carthaginian army would cease to exist as a functional military unit, and with any luck, Hannibal Barca would either be dead upon the battlefield or a prisoner whom Varro could proudly march through the streets of Rome.

Of course, Hannibal had far different ideas. He knew Varro would deploy his army in a formation with the infantry in the center of the line and cavalry on either flank. This formation was the traditional deployment of nearly all of the armies of that time period, and Hannibal would be deploying his own Carthaginian troops in the same fashion, but Hannibal deployed his troops according to the strengths and weaknesses of the various units.

Hannibal would create his line by starting on either flank and positioning his cavalry. While his army overall was significantly smaller than the Roman army (perhaps around 50,000 men compared to Varro's nearly 85,000), the Carthaginian cavalry numbered nearly 10,000, which was 4,000 more than the Roman cavalry. Moreover, these cavalry were more skilled than those that made up Varro's cavalry. The Roman legions relied primarily upon the strength of the heavily armed infantry working in conjunction to win their battles, while the Roman cavalry would be used to turn an enemy's flank by slashing into their unprotected sides and help chase and hunt down fleeing enemy troops. This, however, was not the case with the Carthaginian cavalry, which Hannibal divided into three separate groups. The first two groups were from Hispanic and Celtic tribes respectively. They fought in a brutal and vicious fashion, making up in ferocity what they lacked in grace. The third group consisted of the Numidians.

Hannibal was also fully aware of each infantry unit's individual strengths and weaknesses. With these aspects of his infantry clearly in mind, Hannibal prepared an infantry line that would support his plan and give it the best possible chance of success against the overwhelmingly large force which the Romans, Etruscans, and Samnites had assembled. On the left and right flanks of his infantry line, Hannibal positioned his cavalry to counteract and defeat the Roman cavalry. Then, working in from both the left and the right sides, Hannibal stationed his Iberian heavy infantry units. These were men who were armed and equipped with the gear and weapons of the Roman legionaries whom Hannibal's Carthaginians had already defeated. The Iberians were skilled soldiers and battle-hardened veterans, which meant they were also disciplined. These men would stand, and they would fight.

Meanwhile, the center of the Carthaginian line of battle was made up of men from both Spain and Gaul. While these men were fierce warriors, they were not heavy infantry and were uncomfortable with large set battles. The style of combat with which these men were most familiar was one where they could rapidly strike and then break away. Hannibal had no doubts concerning the courage of these men, but he needed them to be a cohesive force for his plan of double envelopment to work against the Roman army, and with the desire and habit of the Spanish and Gallic warriors to slip away fully in mind, Hannibal set up the Spanish and Gallic units in an alternating fashion. Thus, there would be a Spanish or Gallic unit alongside an Iberian unit, but the Spaniards and Gauls would never be stationed alongside their own compatriots, which Hannibal hoped would ensure no unit could compel nearby countrymen to panic and run. Moreover, the Spanish troops and Gallic troops would feel compelled to outperform one another in order to show that they were the better fighters.

Just as importantly, Hannibal knew that his own presence in the midst of his skittish Spanish and Gallic infantry would serve as a catalyst. Not only would the men seek to outperform one another for the sake of their own honor, they would want to impress their general with their personal bravery and prowess. Hannibal knew this about the men, and thus he sought to act upon it. In addition to his own presence, Hannibal also helped to keep his infantry firm by making sure that he would be able to position his army first upon the field at Cannae. This simple act of arriving first at the scene of the fight to come enabled him to utilize the pros and cons of the ground at Cannae so that they would be beneficial to his tactical goals.

While Varro believed that the position of Hannibal's infantry with the Aufidus River at the rear of the Carthaginian army was a catastrophic mistake, Hannibal obviously did not. Instead, Hannibal knew that his position in front of the river would serve two important purposes that could well give him victory in the battle to come. The first of these purposes was that the Aufidus River's mere presence would serve as a further bulwark to the courage of his Spanish and Gallic infantry. After all, these men knew that if they did break and run, they would eventually be forced to attempt to cross the river, which would put them in extremely vulnerable positions. The Roman legionaries, armed with the pilum (a short javelin), would be able to cut down the fleeing Spanish and Gallic troops at their leisure. Moreover, in addition to strengthening the resolve of the men in the center of his infantry line, Hannibal believed that the position of the Aufidus River at his rear protected him. The Roman troops and cavalry would be unable to attack the rear of his infantry from that position since there were no bridges or easy fords for the Romans to utilize.

What Varro also failed to realize was that the Carthaginian army, by arriving first upon Cannae and being able to choose its position, had tremendous benefits with its back to the Aufidus River. By establishing his force in front of the river, Hannibal ensured the Roman army had a hill at its back. This, in turn, would make any sort of orderly withdrawal from the battlefield difficult should they attempt to do so up the hill. A legionary climbing the hill in full armor and unable to maintain discipline or unit cohesion could be easily killed by Carthaginian cavalry and light infantry. In addition to having the hill behind them, the Romans also had the Aufidus River on their right flank. This hemmed the Roman legions in just as much as Varro believed that the river was trapping the Carthaginians.

Furthermore, Hannibal had stationed his troops in such a way that they stood with the sun behind their backs. With the sun rising behind the Carthaginians, the Roman legions would find that they had to march into the sun's glare, shining not only from the sky but being reflected and magnified by the armor and the weapons of the Carthaginians. The position of the sun, then, partially blinded the approaching Roman infantry and cavalry.

Lastly, Hannibal had noticed that the winds on the day of the battle were blowing in a southeasterly direction. While this fact would potentially mean little to the first few ranks of

Varro's compressed and stacked up legions advancing upon the Carthaginians, it would be misery to others. The following 30-50 rows of Roman legionaries would be forced to deal with the dust and the sand that was stirred up by tens of thousands of marching feet.

Thus, the river, the sun, and the wind all seemed to favor Hannibal and the Carthaginian army at the beginning of that fateful August day.

Chapter 6: The Battle of Cannae

According to the ancient historian Polybius, both sides were forced to begin the battle on a minimum of sleep. This fatigue was a direct result of both the Romans and the Carthaginians having traveled a good distance from their camps to the site of the battle. The Carthaginian army had left their camp earlier than the Romans had so Hannibal could be certain that he and his men would be able to seize the ground that he both wanted and needed, while the Roman legions and their allies had to deal with thirst. The raids by the Carthaginian cavalry on the Roman foragers and water bearers had effectively limited the amount of water available, and this thirst was exacerbated by the dust and sand kicked up by the combatants and subsequently driven steadily into the Roman ranks by the southeasterly wind.

The opening movements of the Battle of Cannae gave no suggestion that it would be one of the most decisive battles in history, but unbeknownst to the Romans, it fit the pattern that Hannibal needed in order to pull off a double envelopment that would crash down upon the Roman line from both flanks and make escape all but impossible. Polybius described the beginning of the fighting: "The battle was begun by an engagement between the advanced guard of the two armies; and at first the affair between these light-armed troops was indecisive. But as soon as the Iberian and Celtic cavalry got at the Romans, the battle began in earnest, and in the true barbaric fashion: for there was none of the usual formal advance and retreat; but when they once got to close quarters, they grappled man to man, and, dismounting from their horses, fought on foot. But when the Carthaginians had got the upper hand in this encounter and killed most of their opponents on the ground,— because the Romans all maintained the fight with spirit and determination,—and began chasing the remainder along the river, slaying as they went and giving no quarter; then the legionaries took the place of the light-armed and closed with the enemy."

With the Roman and allied legions advancing steadily towards the Carthaginian lines, Hannibal placed himself directly in the front and center of his Spanish and Gallic troops. He made sure that all of the men could see him, and from that exposed position he led his Spanish and Gallic units forward while the Iberian heavy infantry – which stood on either flank of the advancing light infantry – remained rooted in place. The Iberians were to serve as walls on either side of the double envelopment that Hannibal was seeking to use, and the steadfast position of these heavy infantrymen would ensure that the Roman legions remained focused upon the center of the Carthaginian line.

As Hannibal and the Spanish and Gallic troops advanced, the far edges of the center remained connected at their junctions with the Iberians. These Spanish and Gallic units remained in place so that as Hannibal and the other units advanced the Carthaginian line started to create a crescent formation. This crescent curved out towards the advancing Roman legionaries so that within a short time only Hannibal and a small portion of the Carthaginian troops with him met the brunt of the initial attack by Varro's legions.

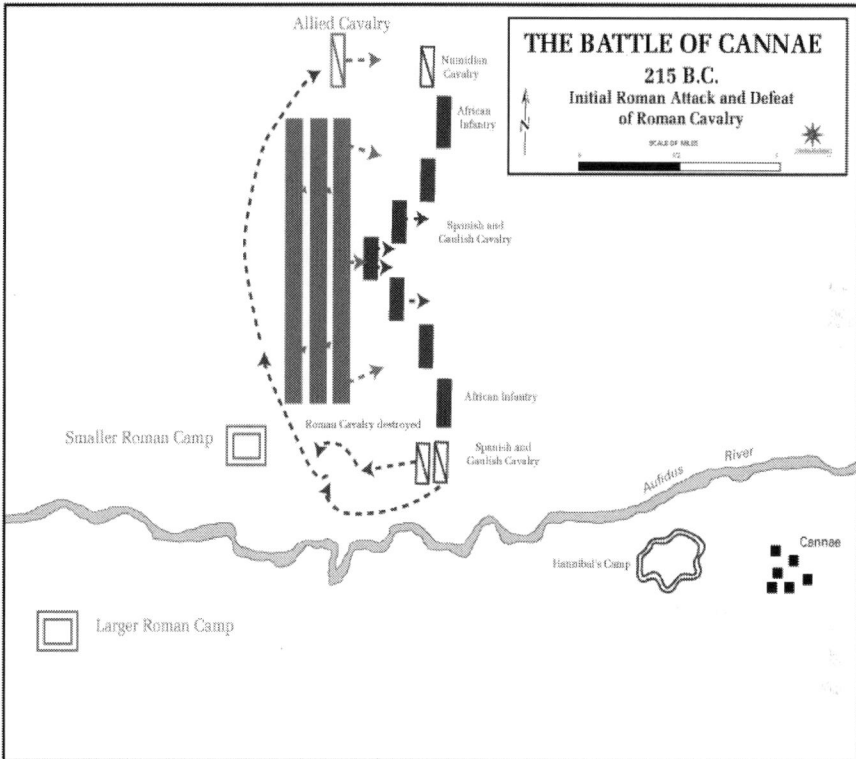

The opening movements at Cannae

Hannibal stayed with his men as the battle ensued, keeping them in a tight formation and encouraging them as they all fell slowly back. None of his Spanish or Gallic troops broke or ran; as Hannibal hoped, they stood beside him and fought even as the Roman legions pushed them backward.

While Hannibal and the Spanish and the Gallic troops steadily fell back, the cavalry of both sides continued to engage one another in combat. On the left flank, nearly 6,500 Hispanic and Celtic cavalry slammed into the Roman and allied cavalry on that flank. Both the Hispanic and the Celtic horsemen dismounted and went about the business of cutting down the legion's cavalry on the left flank. The Carthaginians were ruthless and gave no quarter to the legionaries.

The Numidian cavalry had been positioned on the right flank of the line by Hannibal, and the task of these feared cavalrymen was to keep the Roman cavalry occupied and thus pinned in one place. The Numidians did this by slipping in and out of the Roman cavalry formations, keeping the Romans turned around so that they weren't quite aware of what was going on across the rest of the field.

Shortly after the Hispanic and Celtic cavalry had dispatched the first set, they rode up to the rear of the Roman cavalry, and within a matter of minutes, the Roman cavalry found themselves fighting for their lives on two fronts. The Carthaginian cavalry was attempting to squeeze the Roman cavalry out of existence, and the Roman cavalry quickly fled from the field of Cannae. Polybius described the clash between the cavalry: "Though he had been from the first on the right wing, and had taken part in the cavalry engagement, Lucius Aemilius [Paullus] still survived. Determined to act up to his own exhortatory speech, and seeing that the decision of the battle rested mainly on the legionaries, riding up to the centre of the line he led the charge himself, and personally grappled with the enemy, at the same time cheering on and exhorting his soldiers to the charge. Hannibal, on the other side, did the same, for he too had taken his place on the centre from the commencement. The Numidian horse on the Carthaginian right were meanwhile charging the cavalry on the Roman left; and though, from the peculiar nature of their mode of fighting, they neither inflicted nor received much harm, they yet rendered the enemy's horse useless by keeping them occupied, and charging them first on one side and then on another. But when Hasdrubal, after all but annihilating the cavalry by the river, came from the left to the support of the Numidians, the Roman allied cavalry, seeing his charge approaching, broke and fled."

By the time the Roman cavalry decided that discretion was the better part of valor, Hannibal and his Spanish and the Gallic troops had reversed the crescent. The shape of the center of the Carthaginian line now bowed in, arcing towards the Aufidus River, while the Iberian heavy infantry on either wing still remained steadfast and unengaged. Naturally, the Roman legions, who were stacked up as deeply as 50 men in some places, continued to push and fight forward. Their momentum was impressive, with the men kept in motion by the thousands of men pushing forward from the rear, but as Polybius explained, they were marching right into Hannibal's trap, and when the last ranks of the Roman legions were finally abreast of the Iberians, Hannibal's heavy infantry were in position to execute the pincer on both flanks of the Roman line. "For a short time the Iberian and Celtic lines stood their ground and fought gallantly; but; presently overpowered by the weight of the heavy-armed lines, they gave way and retired to the rear, thus breaking up the crescent. The Roman maniples followed with spirit, and easily cut their way through the enemy's line; since the Celts had been drawn up in a thin line, while the Romans had closed up from the wings towards the centre and the point of danger. For the two wings did not come into action at the same time as the centre: but the centre was first engaged, because the

Gauls, having been stationed on the arc of the crescent, had come into contact with the enemy long before the wings, the convex of the crescent being towards the enemy. The Romans, however, going in pursuit of these troops, and hastily closing in towards the centre and the part of the enemy which was giving ground, advanced so far, that the Libyan heavy-armed troops on either wing got on their flanks. Those on the right, facing to the left, charged from the right upon the Roman flank; while those who were on the left wing faced to the right, and, dressing by the left, charged their right flank,1 the exigency of the moment suggesting to them what they ought to do. Thus it came about, as Hannibal had planned, that the Romans were caught between two hostile lines of Libyans—thanks to their impetuous pursuit of the Celts."

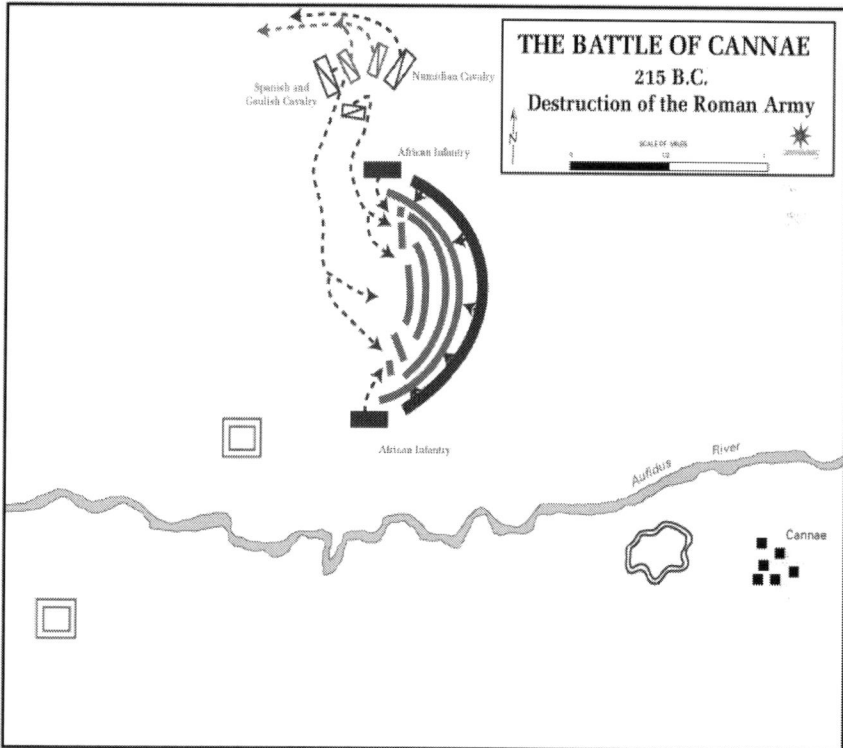

A map depicting the flight of the Roman cavalry and the successful pincer

The Iberian units smashed into each of the unprotected flanks of the massive Roman army, and the tightly packed Roman legionaries could not quickly turn their large, heavy shields in time to protect their lightly armored and nearly unprotected sides. In addition to this sudden attack by the Iberians, the fog of war had already settled upon Cannae, in some cases literally. In addition to the heat of the day and the growing dehydration of the Roman legionaries, the din of battle ensured that the Romans couldn't see what was going on ahead of them thanks to the sand and dust.

Due to these factors, the Roman legionaries would have been completely confused by the sudden presence and sight of the Iberians. As Hannibal's heavy infantry, the Iberians wore the armor and the accouterments of the legionaries themselves, so it would have seemed for at least a moment to the Roman legionaries that they were being attacked by other Romans. Fear would also have been rampant because Varro had arrayed his forces so that the veterans of previous battles and campaigns spearheaded the attack, which left the rear ranks populated with a large number of raw recruits. These men would have been easy for the Iberians to break, especially when the Carthaginian cavalry arrived and effectively sealed off any escape from the rear.

Hannibal and the Spanish and Gallic troops were able to hold the center, and when the Iberians attacked, the forward momentum of Varro's legions was stopped. At this point, the legionaries were still being pressed and pushed forward by the men moving up from their rear, while Hannibal and his men started to push back from the center, the Iberians crashed down on the flanks, and the Carthaginian cavalry swooped in from behind.

The Romans were trapped, their much larger force completely surrounded by a significantly smaller one, and what followed was a complete massacre. Livy captured the desperate straits the Romans had unwittingly put themselves in: "The Carthaginians were driven back and began to withdraw nervously, while the Romans pressed on forward, maintaining the impetus of their attack and driving through the enemy line, which was now in headlong and panic stricken flight. This brought the Romans up against the centre of the Carthaginian position, and then, finding little resistance, against the African reserves. These troops were positioned on both wings, which were drawn back somewhat from the projecting central wedge held by the Gauls and Spanish soldiers. As the wedge was driven back it came level with the main lines of the Carthaginians central position. As they continued to withdraw, the centre of their line became concave, while the African troops on the two wings formed a pair of projecting horns, as it were, gradually enclosing the Roman troops as they charged unthinkingly on against the centre. The Carthaginians rapidly extended their wings and closed in on their opponents from behind. The Romans were now in trouble: their initially successful first assault on the fleeing Gauls and Spaniards had to be abandoned, as they turned to face a new wave of attacks from the Africans behind them. The battle became an unequal struggle for them; they were totally surrounded, and though exhausted, were now compelled to face fresh and vigorous opponents."

According to Polybius, Paullus fell as the Carthaginian cavalry closed in from behind: "At that point Hasdrubal appears to have acted with great skill and discretion. Seeing the Numidians to be strong in numbers, and more effective and formidable to troops that had once been forced from their ground, he left the pursuit [of the Roman cavalry] to them; while he himself hastened to the part of the field where the infantry were engaged, and brought his men up to support the Libyans. Then, by charging the Roman legions on the rear, and harassing them by hurling squadron after squadron upon them at many points at once, he raised the spirits of the Libyans, and dismayed and depressed those of the Romans. It was at this point that Lucius Aemilius fell, in the thick of the fight, covered with wounds: a man who did his duty to his country at that last hour of his life, as he had throughout its previous years, if any man ever did."

Livy gave an even more heroic account of Paullus' death, a clear attempt to create a martyr out of the disaster: "A military tribune called Gnaeus Lentulus was riding past, when he saw the bloodstained consul sitting on a rock. 'Lucius Aemilius Paullus,' he cried, 'you are the only one whom the gods in heaven will hold blameless for today's disaster. Come, take my horse, while there is strength left in your body and I am here to act as your companion, supporter, and defender. Do not desecrate this dreadful battle further with a consul's death. We have cause enough for tears of grief without that.' The consul replied, 'You are a brave man, Gnaeus Cornelius, and a good one. Bless you for it. But you have very little time to escape the enemy's clutches; don't waste it in futile acts of pity. Hurry! Tell the Senate to see to Rome's defences and strengthen them before the victorious enemy arrives. And have a quiet word for me in private with Quintus Fabius. Tell him that as long as I lived and even as I died, I never forgot his words of wisdom. Now leave me here to breathe my last among my slaughtered soldiers. I have no desire to stand trial once again for my consulship, still less to denounce a colleague in the hope that I might protect my own good name by accusing someone else of failure.' As they spoke, a crowd of fugitives raced by, with the enemy in hot pursuit. Without even knowing who he was, they hacked the consul to death, while Lentulus' horse carried him off in the general confusion."

John Trumbull's painting depicting the death of Paullus

Polybius described the end of the battle and the resulting rout:

"As long as the Romans could keep an unbroken front, to turn first in one direction and then in another to meet the assaults of the enemy, they held out; but the outer files of the circle continually falling, and the circle becoming more and more contracted, they at last were all killed on the field; and among them Marcus Atilius and Gnaeus Servilius, the Consuls of the previous year, who had shown themselves brave men and worthy of Rome in the battle. While this struggle and carnage were going on, the Numidian horse were pursuing the fugitives, most of whom they cut down or hurled from their horses; but some few escaped into Venusia, among whom was Gaius Terentius, the Consul, who thus sought a flight, as disgraceful to himself, as his conduct in office had been disastrous to his country.

"Such was the end of the battle of Cannae, in which both sides fought with the most conspicuous gallantry, the conquered no less than the conquerors. This is proved by the fact that, out of six thousand horse, only seventy escaped with Gaius Terentius to Venusia, and about three hundred of the allied cavalry to various towns in the neighbourhood. Of the infantry ten thousand were taken prisoners in fair fight, but were not actually engaged in the battle: of those who were actually engaged only about three thousand perhaps escaped to the towns of the surrounding district; all the rest died nobly, to the number of seventy thousand, the Carthaginians being on this occasion, as on previous ones, mainly indebted for their victory to their superiority in cavalry: a lesson to posterity that in actual war it is better to have half the number of infantry, and the superiority in cavalry, than to engage your enemy with an equality in both. On the side of Hannibal there fell four thousand Celts, fifteen hundred Iberians and Libyans, and about two hundred horse.

"The ten thousand Romans who were captured had not, as I said, been engaged in the actual battle; and the reason was this. Lucius Aemilius left ten thousand infantry in his camp that, in case Hannibal should disregard the safety of his own camp, and take his whole army on to the field, they might seize the opportunity, while the battle was going on, of forcing their way in and capturing the enemy's baggage; or if, on the other hand, Hannibal should, in view of this contingency, leave a guard in his camp, the number of the enemy in the field might thereby be diminished. These men were captured in the following circumstances. Hannibal, as a matter of fact, did leave a sufficient guard in his camp; and as soon as the battle began, the Romans, according to their instructions, assaulted and tried to take those thus left by Hannibal. At first they held their own: but just as they were beginning to waver, Hannibal, who was by this time gaining a victory all along the line, came to their relief, and routing the Romans, shut them up in their own camp; killed two thousand of them; and took all the rest prisoners. In like manner the Numidian horse brought in all those who had taken refuge in the various strongholds about the district, amounting to two thousand of the routed cavalry."

Some historians have estimated that nearly 600 Romans were killed each minute from the beginning of the battle until its end at nightfall. Of the nearly 85,000 Roman and allied troops that fought at Cannae, only an estimated 14,000 of them managed to escape the deft trap Hannibal had sprung. Those 14,000 survivors managed to live by cutting their way out of the trap and making their way to the safe city of Canusium. The rest of the men who did not escape the slaughter remained to fight until they were cut down.

Only darkness brought an end to the killing, but with the coming of daybreak, the Carthaginian soldiers were once more among the Romans. Livy vividly depicted the scene on the field the day after the battle: "Thousands of Roman soldiers lay there, infantry and cavalry scattered everywhere, united in a death which the blind chances of battle or flight had brought upon them. A few, whose wounds had been staunched by the morning frosts, even rose from among the heaps of dead all covered in blood – only to be slaughtered there and then by their enemies. Others were discovered, still alive, but lying there with their knees or hamstrings sliced apart, baring their necks or throats and begging their enemies to drain the rest of their blood. Some were even found with their heads buried in the ground, having dug small pits for themselves and buried their faces in the earth, and then simply smothered themselves to death. The most spectacular sight of all was a Numidian soldier, still alive but lying beneath a dead Roman, with his nose and ears torn to shreds. The Roman had fought to his final breath, and when his hands could no longer hold his weapon, his anger turned to madness, and he died tearing his enemy to pieces with his teeth..."

Most of the Roman wounded were executed, and an estimated 10,000 legionaries were taken prisoner. When the killing of the wounded was finished, nearly 70,000 Roman, Etruscan and Samnite legionaries had been killed at the battle, while Hannibal had lost just 6,000.

Hannibal allowed his victorious men to move amongst the dead, stripping the fallen of everything of use, including weapons, armor, clothing, and rings. Polybius stated that scores of Roman noblemen had fallen in the battle, and all of these men wore the golden rings which marked their status in Roman society. Other rings indicated who among the fallen had been senators. When Hannibal's men were finished stripping rings from the dead, Polybius recorded that the Carthaginians had a bushel full of hundreds of rings.

A statue of Hannibal, with the rings of the Roman nobles he had killed in the battle of Cannae, resting on a Roman standard.

Chapter ?: The Aftermath

A medieval depiction of Cannae

The Battle of Cannae was an unqualified disaster for Rome, unprecedented in the annals of the city, and one with consequences which echoed around the Mediterranean. The Syracusans and Macedonians, now believing that Rome's star was on the wane, abandoned their alliances with the Republic and sided instead with Hannibal. With yet another Roman army decimated, Rome was again at Hannibal's mercy, as Livy noted: "Never before, while the City itself was still safe, had there been such excitement and panic within its walls. I shall not attempt to describe it, nor will I weaken the reality by going into details... it was not wound upon wound but multiplied disaster that was now announced. For according to the reports two consular armies and two consuls were lost; there was no longer any Roman camp, any general, any single soldier in existence; Apulia, Samnium, almost the whole of Italy lay at Hannibal's feet. Certainly there is no other nation that would not have succumbed beneath such a weight of calamity."

In just 20 months, Hannibal had destroyed 3 Roman armies, totaling about 16 legions and upwards of 150,000-200,000 men, and it is estimated that Rome had lost 20% of its adult men. Once again, however, Hannibal inexplicably wavered and opted not to attack Rome itself.

Though he still lacked siege equipment, there would almost certainly have been someone among his allies with expertise in siege warfare, but Hannibal refused to march north, choosing instead to stay in southern Italy. Much of the blame for Hannibal's supineness, in this case, remains with the Carthaginian oligarchy, who once again refused to provide him with money, reinforcements, or the siege equipment he so vitally needed. According to legend, after Cannae, the Numidian cavalry commander Maharbal suggested that Hannibal march on Rome. When Hannibal resisted, Maharbal was alleged to have said, "Truly the Gods have not bestowed all things upon the same person. Thou knowest indeed, Hannibal, how to conquer, but thou knowest not how to make use of your victory." Livy also criticized the great Carthaginian commander for not marching on Rome: "In his moment of victory Hannibal was surrounded by his staff, crowding round to congratulate him and urge him after such a massive success to spend the remainder of the day and the following night resting himself, and giving his exhausted soldiers time to recover. But Maharbal, his cavalry commander would have none of it, urging him not to waste a moment. 'I'll tell you what this battle has really achieved,' he declared, 'when in five days time you are feasting on the Capitol. Follow up quickly. I'll go ahead with the cavalry, and before they even realise we are coming, the Romans will discover we've arrived.' For Hannibal it all seemed far too optimistic, an almost inconceivable possibility. He commended Maharbal for his imaginative idea, but said he needed time to think it through…That single day's delay, by common consent, proved the salvation of Rome and her empire."

Whether Hannibal made the right decision or not, he could certainly have exerted himself a little more. In the event, he chose to capture several cities in southern Italy, and established his headquarters in Capua, one of the richest cities in Southern Italy, which had defected to his side after Cannae, as had much of the southern part of the Italian Peninsula. Hannibal's lassitude during this period, referred to by classical scholars as the "lazings of Capua", is uncharacteristic, but it allowed the Romans to rally. Hannibal contented himself to send a peace delegation to negotiate terms with Rome, but the Senate still refused to deal with Hannibal. Instead, Rome re-dedicated itself to raising more armies and fighting Hannibal.

In the wake of the catastrophe at Cannae, the Roman ruling elite re-evaluated Fabius Maximus' strategy, and began to use his tactics to harass, delay, and whittle down Hannibal's forces in the field, studiously avoiding open battle whenever they could. For years they harried Hannibal's armies, and while there were blunders that allowed Hannibal to lash out (three Roman armies were destroyed in the period between 215 and 212 BCE) the victories were minor and ultimately meaningless. After almost half a decade of continuous warfare, Apulia was a scorched desert incapable of sustaining an army in the field, and Hannibal was getting no supplies either from his allies or from Carthage. Moreover, his allies were proving to be hopelessly ineffective in the field, meaning he either had to lead the force himself or risk losing one of his field armies. Whenever Hannibal did take command, the results were often devastating for Rome, but decisive victory eluded him. Rome could raise far more troops than Hannibal, unsupported, could ever hope to obtain, and a war of attrition was destined to favor them in the end. The tide was finally turning against Hannibal.

In 211, Hannibal received a massive blow as, while his army was in the field, the Romans besieged and captured, with great loss, his base at Capua. Still reeling from this news, his woes were compounded when he discovered that his Syracusan allies had also been crushed, with Sicily fallen to the Romans, and Philip, the king of Macedon, also defeated and driven out of the Roman dominions. Hannibal himself continued to prove himself a great general, inflicting several notable defeats upon all the armies sent against him, but they were, in the long term, meaningless. He fought on, but continued to lose territories throughout 210 and 209 BCE, and between 208 and 207 BCE he was pushed ever southwards, finally being forced to retire to Apulia, where he anxiously awaited reinforcements under the command of his brother, Hasdrubal. At the eleventh hour, these reinforcements might have turned the tide, for once he had the troops at his command Hannibal planned to march upon Rome once and for all. However, Hasdrubal never reached Hannibal. He got himself entangled in a battle with the Romans on the Metaurus, and his army was defeated and he himself killed. Hannibal, knowing his situation in Apulia was untenable, was forced to retreat into Bruttium, the southernmost tip of the Italian peninsula, where he was also forced to endure the horror of having his brother's severed head tossed over the walls and into his camp.

For all intents and purposes, Hannibal's campaign in Italy was over. He succeeded in holding on in Bruttium for a further four years, but was never able to push northward and his army was fast dwindling to nothing, with his veterans being killed off and his mercenaries melting away. In 206 BCE, it was reported to him that Roman armies had occupied the entirety of Iberia, driving the Carthaginian forces from the peninsula, a victory obtained by his old enemy Scipio Africanus, who had utterly crushed the Carthaginians at Ilipa. Finally, in 203 BCE, he was peremptorily recalled to Carthage, 15 years and scores of victories after he had first entered Italy in arms. The reason for his recall was simple: Rome was on the march. A massive army, under the command of Scipio "Africanus", the General whose bravery had saved his eponymous father's life at the beginning of Hannibal's Italian campaign, was preparing to attack and destroy Carthage. Rome wanted revenge.

While Hannibal had been in Italy, it had been relatively easy for the Carthaginian oligarchy, particularly the Hundred and Four, a federation of powerful traders, and Hannibal's chief political rival, Hanno the Great, to marginalize him. For years his political party, the Barcids, had struggled to obtain even a token amount of funds and troops for his enterprise, but Hannibal's arrival on the scene changed all that. Even his rivals could not deny the simple fact that, all else aside, the man could fight a battle like no other general alive. With Rome threatening invasion, Hannibal was suddenly the necessary hero of the hour. Bolstering his Italian mercenaries with levies from Africa and Carthage, the Carthaginian ruling elite desperately invested the money that Hannibal had begged for throughout the last decade in order to assemble a scratch force capable of at least presenting an appearance of force against Scipio Africanus' army.

Hannibal can hardly have been thrilled to see the amount of trouble the Carthaginians went to in order to assemble an army that, had he had his way years before, might well have been completely unnecessary. Certainly it appears that he prepared to take the field with less than his customary ardor. At 45, he was still far from old, but ever since he had first left Carthage he had spent virtually all of his adult life fighting, and the strain was beginning to tell. By all accounts he was in poor health, and prone to sickness. Indeed, rather than seek to bring Scipio Africanus to battle, in 202 BCE Hannibal met the Roman general and attempted to talk peace. The army the Carthaginians had succeeded in gathering, not to mention the presence of Hannibal himself, convinced Scipio that he might be well-advised to seek a diplomatic solution, and the two began negotiations, which were helped by the fact that both generals recognized a kindred spirit in the other. Through negotiations, Carthage was forced to give up much, especially considering Hannibal's roster of victories, but Rome's star was on the rise once again, and Hannibal knew he could not hope to win a protracted war.

Hannibal agreed to Scipio's terms: Carthage would lose possession of Iberia and the Mediterranean islands, renouncing all claims to overseas territories but maintaining its heartland and African possessions, with the exception of the Numidian kingdom of Masinissa, who had declared for Rome. Reparations would be made, Scipio demanded, to Rome itself and to the countless families which Carthage's wars had decimated, and the Carthaginian army and fleet must both be reduced in numbers, in order for them to never again threaten Rome's supremacy. Hannibal, who recognized these terms, though harsh, as probably the best deal Carthage was likely to achieve, acceded to them, but the proposed peace between he and Scipio never happened. While the negotiations were going on, a Roman fleet which had gotten itself stranded upon the coast of Tunisia was seized by the Carthaginian navy and ransacked of all its supplies and equipment. When Scipio heard of this, he furiously demanded reparations, but, unaccountably, the Carthaginian oligarchy high-handedly turned him down. Perhaps they felt secure enough with Hannibal at the head of an army on Carthaginian soil to defy Rome, or perhaps the terms of the treaty stung their pride. Whatever their reasons, they could not have committed a bigger diplomatic error if they had gone out of their way to do so. Scipio departed the negotiations in a rage. There would be no terms.

Engraving of the Battle of Zama

On October 19th, 202 BC, on the plain of Zama, in modern Tunisia, battle was joined. Scipio Africanus led 34,000 Roman legionary infantry, including veteran survivors of Cannae, who had a score to settle with Hannibal, and 9,000 crack Numidian cavalry (the same heavy horse which Hannibal's general Maharbal had used to such devastating effect against the Romans for two decades). Hannibal himself marched to stop him with 45,000 Italian, Iberian, Gaulish and North African infantry (both mercenary and levied), 4,000 cavalry, and around 80 war elephants. For the first time in one of the battles of the Second Punic War, Hannibal had the infantry advantage and Rome had the cavalry advantage.

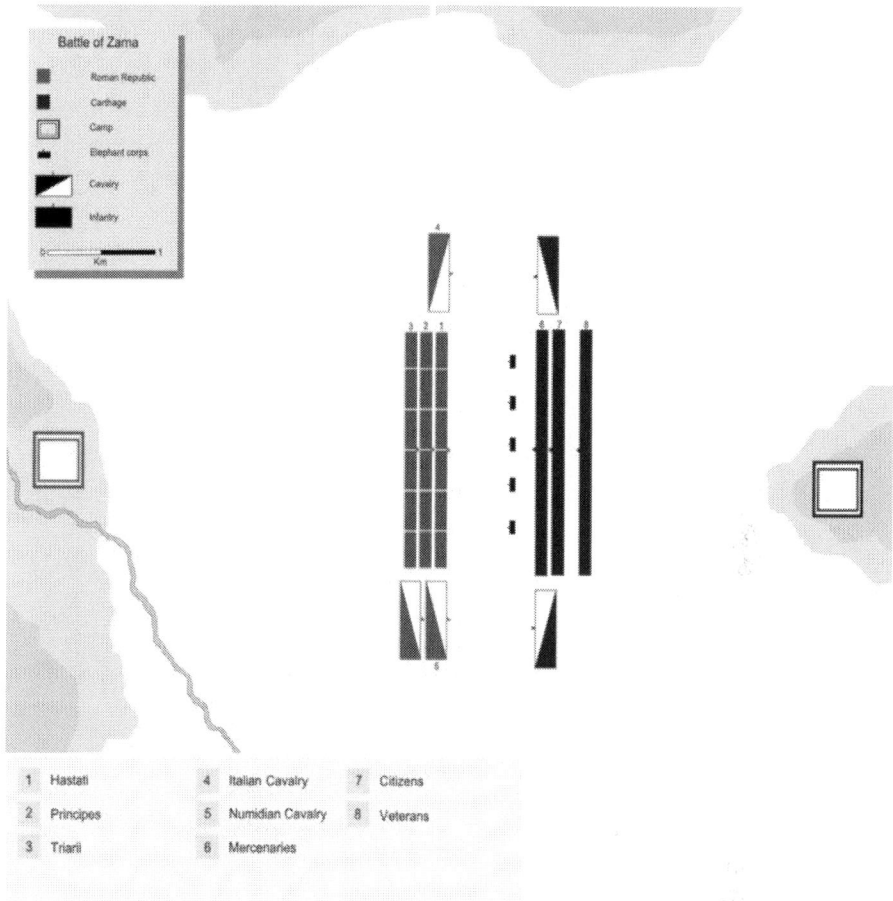

Battle of Zama

	Roman Republic
	Carthage
	Camp
	Elephant corps
	Cavalry
	Infantry

1	Hastati	4	Italian Cavalry	7	Citizens
2	Principes	5	Numidian Cavalry	8	Veterans
3	Triarii	6	Mercenaries		

Hannibal deployed his cavalry on the wings, then placed three lines of infantry, with his Italian veterans in reserve, behind his war elephants, which were to be his secret weapon. Scipio countered by placing his own infantry in three lines, with his veteran heavy infantry in reserve and his own cavalry, which outnumbered Hannibal's by more than two to one, on the flanks. Hannibal opened the battle by pushing forward his war elephants and light infantry, but Scipio checked their advance before they could smash into his battle-lines by unleashing a cloud of skirmishers who harried the elephants with storms of arrows and javelins, while the Roman cavalry blew trumpets to confuse and frighten the elephants, several of which turned the way they had come and charged into the Carthaginian left flank, creating chaos there. Scipio also intentionally opened gaps in his own line for the elephants to drive through harmlessly. Masinissa took advantage of this to charge home against the cavalry on that flank and drive it from the field, but he found himself embroiled in a chase orchestrated on the fly by Hannibal as the Carthaginian cavalry lured him away from the main battle.

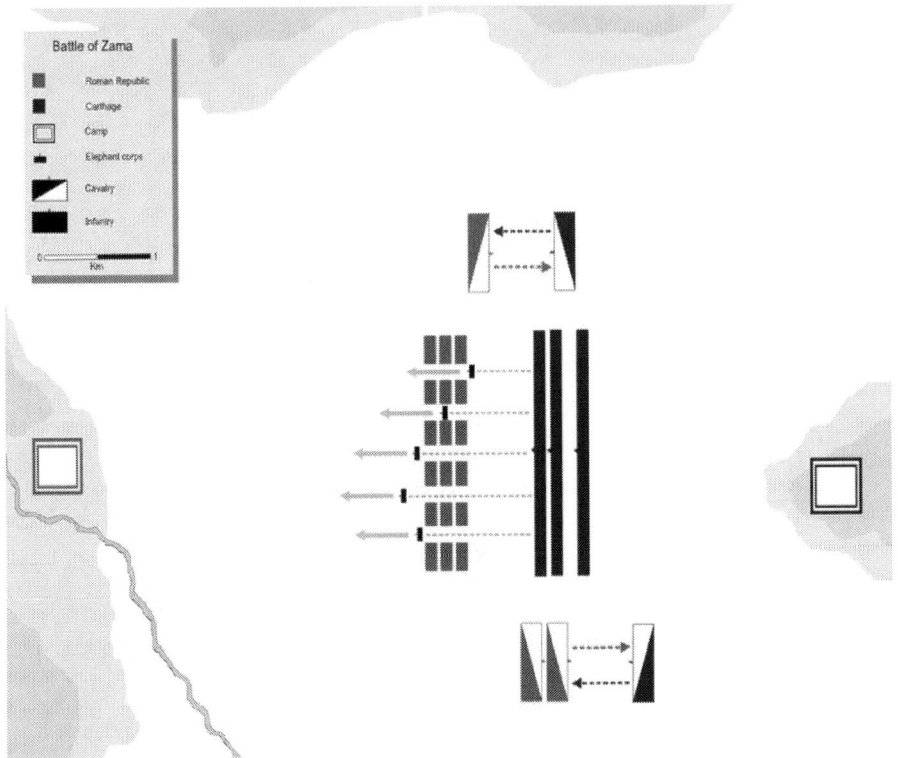

Battle of Zama

Roman Republic
Carthage
Camp
Elephant corps
Cavalry
Infantry

0   1
Km

Meanwhile, the Roman and Carthaginian infantry were hammering each other in the center of the battle-line, with both sides momentarily gaining the advantage, only to be driven back in turn. The battle raged for hours, with neither side able to gain the upper hand, but eventually Masinissa, who had chased the Carthaginian cavalry clean off the field with his superior numbers, returned and charged the Carthaginian forces from behind, enveloping them. Scipio rallied his faltering and exhausted troops to one last great effort and they fell upon the Carthaginian troops, which were trapped and unable to maneuver.

Like Hannibal's masterpiece at Cannae, but this time with the roles inverted, the encircled force had nowhere to run. Thousands were cut down where they stood, with only around a tenth of Hannibal's original force, including Hannibal himself, succeeding in breaking free and escaping. For Carthage, the battle was an utter catastrophe, with over 20,000 dead and 20,000 taken prisoner, most of which were grievously wounded. Hannibal's first defeat was so dire that he lost all credibility in Carthage, and his enemies used it to blacken his reputation and forced him to surrender his generalship. With no army in the field, Carthage sued for peace, at far more costly terms than those which they could have accepted with no further loss of life.

Now that Carthage had surrendered virtually all military ambition, Hannibal himself devoted himself to politics. He secured his election to chief magistrate through the support of the Barcid party and introduced highly successful political and financial reforms, much to the chagrin of his rivals. Hannibal was so successful as a politician that Carthage, despite still being hampered by a heavy war indemnity, prospered to the point that the Romans demanded he step down as magistrate. Rather than do so, Hannibal voluntarily went into exile, worried he might expose Carthage to new Roman reprisals.

For the next eight years he was received as a mercenary commander at many middle-eastern courts, particularly at the court of Antiochus of Syria, in Ephesus, who was preparing for an invasion of Italy. Hannibal, ever conscious of his oath to his father, offered to take command of Antiochus's troops, but Antiochus declined the offer and was soundly beaten the following year. Antiochus, seeking a scapegoat, blamed Hannibal and proposed to sell him to the Romans, prompting him to move yet again. Strabo and Plutarch both wrote that Hannibal spent some time at the court of Artaxias I, and he eventually made his way back to Asia Minor and fought with Prusias I of Bithynia against King Eumenes II of Pergamon, a Roman ally. It was said that during one naval battle, Hannibal devised the idea of filling large pots with venomous snakes and throwing them onto the enemies' ships, wreaking havoc. After Hannibal defeated Eumenes in a couple of land battles, Rome demanded that Bythinia surrender Hannibal to them. The frightened Prusias complied, but Hannibal was determined not to let himself be taken alive and poisoned himself at Lybissa, in Asia Minor, in 183 BCE Roman historians speculated he had long carried the poison in a ring in case he needed to use it in battle, but poison kept that long might very well no longer be effective. In any case, Hannibal left a letter behind which dryly remarked that his death should provide some comfort to the Romans by relieving them of the fear they had felt for so long, since they apparently could not abide waiting patiently for an old man to die. "Let us relieve the Romans from the anxiety they have so long experienced, since they think it tries their patience too much to wait for an old man's death."

Despite Hannibal's incredible success in Italy, Carthage was on the brink of death by the end of the Second Punic War, but it swiftly proved once again that it was nothing if not resourceful. Despite having been humbled and reduced virtually to city-state status, Carthage quickly recovered economically by taking advantage of the privileged trading position which had been the backbone of her wealth since her foundation. Interestingly, the ruthless demilitarization imposed by the Romans upon the Carthaginians actually aided the city's economic redevelopment; since Carthage no longer had to pay to maintain vast mercenary armies at home or abroad, their defense budget was virtually nonexistent.

Over the next five decades, Carthage slowly rebuilt her economy and even prospered, causing much annoyance and some alarm in Rome. However, ever since the defeat at Cannae, Massinissa's Numidians had raided across the new Carthaginian border with impunity, and since Carthage lacked a standing army she was forced to bring any grievances she might have before the Roman Senate, where Punic complaints were generally overruled as a matter of principle.

Carthage eventually responded by refusing to pay the annual tribute to Rome and raising an army, which they launched in a retaliatory raid against Massinissa, only to promptly be defeated by the Numidians.

This behavior alarmed much of the Roman political establishment, including the famous orator Cato the Elder, who began to end all of his speeches, regardless of their subject matter, by urging the destruction of Carthage. In his biography of Cato the Elder, Plutarch wrote:

> "Some will have the overthrow of Carthage to have been one of his last acts of state; when, indeed, Scipio the younger did by his velour give it the last blow, but the war, chiefly by the counsel and advice of Cato, was undertaken on the following occasion. Cato was sent to the Carthaginians and Masinissa, King of Numidia, who were at war with one another, to know the cause of their difference. He, it seems, had been a friend of the Romans from the beginning; and they, too, since they were conquered by Scipio, were of the Roman confederacy, having been shorn of their power by loss of territory and a heavy tax. Finding Carthage, not (as the Romans thought) low and in an ill condition, but well manned, full of riches and all sorts of arms and ammunition, and perceiving the Carthaginians carry it high, he conceived that it was not a time for the Romans to adjust affairs between them and Masinissa; but rather that they themselves would fall into danger, unless they should find means to check this rapid new growth of Rome's ancient irreconcilable enemy. Therefore, returning quickly to Rome, he acquainted the senate that the former defeats and blows given to the Carthaginians had not so much diminished their strength, as it had abated their imprudence and folly; that they were not become weaker, but more experienced in war, and did only skirmish with the Numidians to exercise themselves the better to cope with the Romans: that the peace and league they had made was but a kind of suspension of war which awaited a fairer opportunity to break out again.

> Moreover, they say that, shaking his gown, he took occasion to let drop some African figs before the senate. And on their admiring the size and beauty of them, he presently added, that the place that bore them was but three days' sail from Rome. Nay, he never after this gave his opinion, but at the end he would be sure to come out with this sentence, 'ALSO, CARTHAGE, METHINKS, OUGHT UTTERLY TO BE Destroyed.' But Publius Scipio Nasica would always declare his opinion to the contrary, in these words, 'It seems requisite to me that Carthage should still stand.' For seeing his countrymen to be grown wanton and insolent, and the people made, by their prosperity, obstinate and disobedient to the senate, and drawing the whole city, whither they would, after them, he would have had the fear of Carthage to serve as a bit to hold the

contumacy of the multitude; and he looked upon the Carthaginians as too weak to overcome the Romans, and too great to be despised by them. On the other side, it seemed a perilous thing to Cato that a city which had been always great, and was now grown sober and wise, by reason of its former calamities, should still lie, as it were, in wait for the follies and dangerous excesses of the over-powerful Roman people; so that he thought it the wisest course to have all outward dangers removed, when they had so many inward ones among themselves.

Thus Cato, they say, stirred up the third and last war against the Carthaginians: but no sooner was the said war begun, than he died, prophesying of the person that should put an end to it who was then only a young man"

Ancient bust of Cato the Elder

Matters ultimately did come to a head in 149 BCE, when Rome, tired of Carthaginian resurgence and seeking a pretext for invasion, first demanded that hundreds of children from Carthaginian noble families be handed over as hostages. When it seemed as though the

Carthaginians might actually accede to this condition, the Romans ordered Carthage to be demolished and the entire city rebuilt inland away from the coast. The Carthaginians, unsurprisingly, told the Senate this was unacceptable, after which Rome promptly declared war.

A Roman fleet carrying 80,000 infantry and 4,000 cavalry landed in North Africa, depositing the troops near the Carthaginian city of Utica. This Roman force represented 20 legions of disciplined Roman legionaries, and they were camped only 10 miles from the city of Carthage. The presence of this force, combined with the failure of the Romans to control the Numidians and the Roman Senate's harsh demands, ensured a change in the Carthaginian government; the party which had so long sought to appease Rome following the end of the Second Punic War was replaced and a government which sought to fight the Romans and retain their Carthaginian pride came into power following the Roman demand that Carthage be abandoned.

The Roman army and fleet did not attack the Carthaginians immediately after Carthage's refusal to comply to the last demand to abandon the city, and this waiting period proved to be exceptionally costly for the Roman legions. The legions were struck down with disease, after which the combat ready legionaries were so few in number that the Roman command was unable to launch any sort of attack against the city of Carthage.

While the Roman army sough to heal itself and prepare for a vigorous campaign against Carthage, the Carthaginians were seemingly trapped within the walls of Carthage. The Romans had underestimated the tenacity of the Carthaginians, however. With 20 Roman legions a mere 10 miles from them, the Carthaginian people transformed their temples into workshops for the fabrication of weapons and armor. It was said that the Carthaginian women even went so far as to cut short their hair, and the shorn locks were twisted into cord for use as bowstrings. Thus, while the Romans sought to bring their legions back up to their peak physical condition, the Carthaginians proposed to defend themselves from the inevitable siege and gathered food and supplies.

After the passing of several months the Romans were ready to begin what they believed would be a short and successful siege. The Roman legions were divided into two commands. The first section was commanded by consul Manius Manilius, whose command consisted of the greater portion of the infantry and cavalry. His plan of attack was to cross an isthmus which separated the cities of Utica and Carthage, and upon crossing the isthmus, he would have the legions fill in the protective ditch surrounding the city of Carthage. With this impediment taken care of, he would have his legions move on to the first of two walls. The first was a low parapet which his legions would easily be able to climb, and the second was the high wall which protected the city itself. Siege engines and scaling equipment would be used to breach the high wall and attack the unprotected city.

The second wing of the Roman attack would come in the form of an attack by sea, which would be led by consul Lucius Marcius Censorinus. Censorinus would sail the Roman fleet up to the unprotected sea wall of Carthage. Some of his troops would disembark, and together the ground troops and seaborne troops would assault the city. The landed infantry and the seaborne troops would both use scaling ladders to assault the wall in conjunction with Manilius' assault on the city's front.

Once the plan of attack was agreed upon and in place, both Manius Manilius and Lucius Marcius Censorinus launched their attacks on the city. Neither of the consuls expected there to be any sort of resistance from the Carthaginians, as both men knew that the city had been unable to send out for arms, armor and assistance. Of course, both of the consuls had failed to take into consideration the fact that the Carthaginians might well have found a way to defend themselves against a Roman attack they knew was coming.

When the combined attack occurred, the consuls were horrified by the fierce, desperate resistance of the Carthaginians to the Roman attack. Confused and disorientated, the legions fell back; their first assault on Carthage had been an unequivocal failure. Having been disabused of the notion that the conquest would be easy, the consuls fell back and regrouped their forces. The consuls struck at the city once more, but again the Romans were repelled by the Carthaginians and had to fall back well away from the city.

At this point the Roman consuls became worried. Carthage would not simply surrender itself to Rome, and they were worried about forces under the Carthaginian commander Hasdrubal, who had positioned himself behind the Romans on the opposite side of a lake. He fortified his positions and looked for opportunities to strike at the Roman legions, and one came when engineers attached to Censorinus' command entered the woods around the lake. The task that they sought to accomplish was the harvesting of wood to build larger siege engines for a renewed assault upon Carthage, but while the engineers were directing the gathering of wood, a small force of Carthaginians under the command of Himilco Phameas fell upon them.

Despite the attack, the engineers, while suffering a large loss of men, were still able to gather enough wood for the siege engines, and with this wood, Censorinus and Manilius constructed new engines and ladders for a third assault upon the city of Carthage. This attack took place with both groups of legions operating in conjunction with the other, but this third attempt was still beaten back.

After this failure, Manilius focused on the fortifications in the front of the city, but even here the Carthaginians were able to successfully beat back the Roman assaults. Eventually, Manilius became despondent and lacked any belief that the Roman legions would ever succeed in breaking through the walls of Carthage.

While Manilius suffered from a lack of faith, Lucius Marius Censorinus did not. Rather than bemoaning the fate of the legions in front of Carthage, Censorinus prepared for another attempt to break into the city. Using Roman perseverance, Censorinus had his legions fill in a portion of the lake next to Carthage, and when that was done, he had a wider space with which he could assault the Carthaginian walls. Using two large battering rams, his troops finally succeeded in breaking the wall, but when they attempted to make use of the breach and gain the city, they were beaten back by the Carthaginians. When night descended, the Carthaginians started to rebuild the wall.

Although they repaired the wall, the Carthaginians also realized that the work would be insufficient to stop the Roman battering rams. What followed was an example of Carthaginian heroism and determination. Under the cover of darkness, a group of Carthaginians attacked the Romans through the breach in the city wall in order to destroy the battering rams. The lightly armed forces were rapidly beaten back by the Roman forces, but not before disabling the battering rams and rendering them useless until the Romans could repair them.

When day dawned, the Roman legionaries saw that the Carthaginians, armed solely with clubs and stones, stood in the small courtyard open to the breach. The Carthaginians lined the courtyard, the roofs, and the walls and waited for the legionaries. The commander of the Roman troops at the breach was a young tribune by the name of Publius Cornelius Scipio Aemilianus. Instead of having his troops rush headlong into the breach, he stationed groups of men along either side of the breach and then ordered a unit of legionaries into the city.

The Carthaginians were ferocious in their defense of the city, and once again the legionaries were driven back and out of the breach. Had Aemilianus not stationed troops on either side of the breach, the Carthaginians may have succeeded in annihilating the Roman forces altogether, and as a result, Aemilianus' actions came to the attention of the commanders.

Shortly after this, before the Roman consuls could prepare the legions for another assault on Carthage, widespread illnesses began to sweep the ranks once more. With the troops sick, Censorinus took his command post out of the fleet, which sat off of the port side of Carthage, and began to plot his next move. The Carthaginians, however, had already began to act upon theirs. Since the winds were blowing towards the Roman fleet, people within the city prepared a large group of fire boats. These vessels were filled with tinder and flammables before being carried through the city to a corner of the city wall which protruded into the sea. With the wall serving as a shield from Roman eyes, the Carthaginians lowered the boats into the water and raised the sails, and as the wind started to drive the boats around the wall and towards the Roman fleet, the Carthaginians poured both pitch and brimstone onto the boats from atop the walls and lit them. The wind drove the boats furiously into the Roman ships, lighting them on fire, and the tactic proved so effective that Rome lost nearly the entire fleet anchored off of Carthage's walls.

After the loss of the fleet, Censorinus returned to Rome, both to report on the status of the war and to take care of the political necessity of conducting an election to retain his position as consul. Meanwhile, Manilius stayed within his camp outside of the city. The Carthaginians, however, did not remain within the city. Shortly after Censorius' departure for Rome the

Carthaginians made a night assault upon the Roman camp. Mostly unarmed, the Carthaginian troops carried wooden planks with which to cross the ditch which surrounded the Roman camp, and after crossing the trench the Carthaginians attempted to destroy the Roman fortifications.

As the Carthaginians assaulted the front of the encampment, Aemilianus exited the camp via the rear upon his horse and charged the Carthaginians from the flank. Due to the inevitable confusion of night combat, the Carthaginians believed that the young tribune was at the head of a larger force and retreated to the sanctuary of Carthage. As the war progressed Aemilianus' name gained more recognition and renown.

Aemilianus continued making a good name for himself, and in addition to his bravery, he was known for his ability to use subterfuge and trickery when necessary. Such an incident occurred when the Carthaginians launched another attack upon Manilius' camp, this time from the sea at night. While Manilius chose to keep his troops within the walls, Aemilianus led a large group of cavalry out onto the field where the Carthaginians were gathered and assaulting the fortifications. By ordering his cavalry to carry only lit torches and to not engage the Carthaginians, and by having the cavalry ride around the enemy yelling and waving their torches, Aemilianus was able to force the Carthaginian to withdraw in confusion.

While the Carthaginians continued to hold out against the Roman siege, Manilius left his encampment with two legions to seek an engagement with a roving Carthaginian force commanded by Hasdrubal. However, Manilius' timidity and lack of tactical knowledge led him to make several poor decisions which Aemilianus attempted to turn the consul from. Undeterred, Manilius proceeded into a narrow valley, allowing Hasdrubal to ambush the two legions, but in the fighting that followed, Aemilianus took command of a large group of cavalry and effectively enabled the defeated legions to withdraw. When it was later discovered that four cohorts of the legions had been left behind, dug in yet surrounded, Aemilianus again took the initiative and with his cavalry achieved what was believed to be impossible by breaking the hold of Hasdrubal's forces around the four cohorts, driving the Carthaginians from the field, and rescuing the trapped legionaries.

Shortly after this incident, Aemilianus returned to Rome and sought out a consul seat. Many of the men with whom he had served in North Africa wrote home that Aemilianus alone could destroy Carthage. Even the consul Manilius, shortly before being replaced, sent word to Rome that Aemilianus should return to North Africa, not as a tribune but as consul, in order to bring an end to the Carthaginians.

By December of 148 BCE, the citizens of Rome had grown tired of the war already. They had also heard of Aemilianus' exploits in North Africa, so when the time to vote came, he was awarded a consul position. In addition to this, he was given North Africa as his province so that he might command the legions. The Roman public also gave him the right to conscript men into service to replace those who had already been lost in the war.

Thus, in the spring of 147 BCE, Aemilianus gathered his troops and sailed for the Carthaginian city of Utica. Meanwhile, the Romans in North Africa continued to push against the Carthaginian defenses. From the spring of 147 to the spring of 146, Aemilianus drove his forces through the Carthaginian territories, restoring discipline to the legions, capturing Carthaginian positions of strength, and stopping supplies from reaching Carthage.

Finally, as the spring of 146 neared its end, Aemilianus attacked the city of Carthage. The Carthaginians, weak from nearly three years of siege warfare, disease, and lack of supplies, were unable to defend their walls when the Romans attacked. As the legionaries poured into the city, a brutal form of fighting began from street to street and house to house. For seven days, the Romans and Carthaginians engaged in brutal urban warfare, but Rome was victorious in the end. Only 50,000 of Carthage's citizens survived, and these people were sold into slavery. For 17 days the Romans burned the city to the ground, and those buildings that remained were torn down by hand so that nothing of the city remained.

A picture of the excavated ruins of Ancient Carthage

The Third Punic War marked the end of Carthage as any sort of city or people, and it allowed Rome to continue its rise to power within the Mediterranean. Rome's ability to soundly defeat an enemy regardless of its location was a factor for new enemies and possible challengers alike to consider.

Online Resources

Other books about Ancient Rome by Charles River Editors

Other books about the Punic Wars on Amazon

Bibliography

Bagnall, Nigel (1990). The Punic Wars. ISBN 0-312-34214-4.

Daly, Gregory. Cannae: The Experience of Battle in the Second Punic War. London/New York: Routledge, ISBN 0-415-32743-1.

Delbrück, Hans. Warfare in Antiquity, 1920, ISBN 0-8032-9199-X.

Goldsworthy, Adrian (2006). The Fall of Carthage. ISBN 978-03043-6642-2.

Lazenby, John Francis (1978). Hannibal's War. ISBN 978-0-8061-3004-0.

Lancel, Serge (1995). Hannibal (in French).

Polybius, Histories, Evelyn S. Shuckburgh (translator); London, New York. Macmillan (1889); Reprint Bloomington (1962).

Palmer, Robert E. A. (1997). Rome and Carthage at Peace. Stuttgart.

Mahaney, W.C, 2008. "Hannibal's Odyssey, Environmental Background to the Alpine Invasion of Italia," Gorgias Press, Piscataway, N.J, 221 pp.

Dodge, Theodore Ayrault (1891). Hannibal. Reprinted by Da Capo Press, Cambridge, Mass. ISBN 0-306-81362-9

Printed in Great Britain
by Amazon